THE PSYCHOLOGY OF THE ACTOR

The Psychology of the Actor

YOTI LANE

THE JOHN DAY COMPANY • NEW YORK

CONTENTS

INTRODUCTION

One of the most tragic aspects of the acting profession is its tremendous waste of human material. This waste is obvious, not only in the world of the theatre itself but in the dramatic schools and drama classes which are the portals to that world. Many students go through a two-year course and then never obtain an engagement—an experience likely to inflict permanent psychic injury on a young and impressionable mind. Many more struggle along for years in obscurity, despite considerable talents, for lack of some quality necessary to achieve their goal.

After many years as a producer and teacher of drama I found myself becoming more and more engrossed with this problem. Gradually I came to realize that if many of the stage-struck youngsters who crowd eagerly into the dramatic schools each year had understood themselves better, they might never have sought stage careers; and that those who failed after passing through the dramatic school might have fared better if they had had any real knowledge of the psychology of the actor.

7

Although it has long been recognized that people who make good doctors have certain psychological characteristics in common, it is not usually realized that this is true of actors also; as a result, little attempt has been made to analyze the characteristics which good actors share and need for success. I am not referring to abilities to give a performance. There is a misleading popular conception of "the actor." People who know little of acting will often point to some friend who "should be on the stage": but those friends are usually extroverts with a talent for mimicry, whereas the good actor, as often as not, is a very retiring and even introverted personality when not on the stage.

A youngster who tries to enter the theatrical profession is gambling his (or her) whole future, for the failed actor has even less chance of settling down happily in some other career than the failed priest. Both actors and priests have to become dedicated men, and the would-be actor should be handled in much the same way as the young man who has a vocation for the priesthood. The would-be priest is put through a long process of psychological testing before being accepted into a seminary; unfortunately, the would-be actor can enter a drama school without any such attempt being made to test his real suitability for the profession—he requires little more than the ability to give a reasonable and audible audition, and to accept what he is taught.

In this book I have tried to analyze the characteristics that are shared by most successful actors and to trace these distinguishing traits back to the early environmental forces which molded or developed them. My material comes from records of the progress of individual students, from knowledge of their subsequent careers, and from the answers a large number of them gave to a questionnaire I compiled. I also discussed the distinctive qualities of actors with a number of professional friends, and considered their answers to the questionnaire. In addition, I was enabled to conduct a survey. Several hundred players contacted me and obtained copies of the questionnaire, which they filled in and returned.

Finally, I submitted my conclusions to a well-known psychiatrist, who was in complete agreement with them.

I hope that this book will interest not only those who are thinking of going on the stage and those who have begun their careers, but all who love that looking-glass world where magic is generated—the theatre.

YOTI LANE

THE PSYCHOLOGY OF THE ACTOR

CHAPTER one

IN THE BEGINNING

Among the first professional actors were tribal Ju-Ju men or witch doctors. Much later, in ancient Greece, came the priests of the temple of Dionysius with the chanting of choric hymns as part of their ritual. Later they introduced instrumental music into their ceremonies, dancing and speech followed. Out of this came the theatre and the performance of secular drama. There were professional actors as we know them today, popular favorites with large followings.

Greece declined as a great power and Roman imperialism took its place. Theatrical entertainment continued to develop and the Romans built theatres in many of their colonies.

After the fall of the Roman Empire the theatre suffered a decline, but it revived with the growth of Christian civilization. In an age of mass ignorance and illiteracy theatrical performances of simple religious dramas were an ideal means of imparting education in the new religion.

13

The Church needed the theatre and the theatre needed the Church, not only for the protection it offered but because the church buildings were the only premises suitable for theatrical performances.

In early medieval society there was little scope for individual effort or enterprise and man scarcely existed as an individual. He lived very much as a member of a group, and as a group, theatrical performers were not powerful enough to exist without the patronage and protection of the Church.

Medieval economy was more stable than that of modern times, partly because humble and powerful alike believed that their place in life was divinely ordained—one man was born a noble, another a toiler. A man who followed the trade of his father or who was fortunate enough to be apprenticed to a trade was sure of his social and economic position for the rest of his life. For the person who was competent at his trade there were, within strict limits, both security and opportunity. So around the churches in the larger communities little groups of players grew and became established. There were no famous actors among them because there was little incentive to aspire to any unique distinction (except in less important matters) so that players worked as a team. However, no art can remain static and survive. Gradually into the lines and situations of the plays there came a new trend. No one knows the name of the first dramatist to criticize or at least satirize Church and State, but he goes back a long way. By the fourteenth century the Church began to take exception to certain aspects of the plays performed. In the course of time the players were driven from the interior of the churches to the steps, and from there to the booth, the market square and the innyard.

Although the first threat to the security of the medieval

theatre had come from within, a much greater threat was approaching from the outside world. While feudalism had fostered stability, it hindered expansion. Great markets were opening up and the exploitation of these markets demanded fluid capital; money was potentially more valuable than a vast reservoir of serfs.

When feudalism came to an end, the old way of life—interpreted as a God-ordained pattern—was gone and man's relationship to himself and others drastically changed. He could no longer live according to a communal plan but was an individual with certain freedoms, including the freedom to starve. The comfort, as well as the confinement of being one of a tightly organized social body, was gone forever. He now had to think, act and fight for survival for himself and those dependent upon him. Since the mass of the people were poor and wanting in knowledge, many were ill-equipped for the struggle. The Renaissance gave release to man's creative forces, but at the same time it contributed to his sense of insecurity which, with the passing of the centuries, has increased rather than abated.

In some ways the actor in the new world of the Renaissance was more fortunate than many other people. If he had talent and initiative he had greater scope to develop than ever before and because his profession demanded that he live in a closely knit group he escaped isolation. He also had the good fortune that his group differed from others' groups. Even today a company of actors—however individualistic they may be—are people whose similarities are greater than their diversities. Also, it was still accepted that companies of players should rely on patronage to a very great extent. Plays were performed in the castles or palaces of patrons and a good picture of their way of life is provided in the Players scene in Shakespeare's *Hamlet*.

Theatrical programs were varied and usually included singing, dancing and mime as well as short plays. In many European countries music and singing occupied a good deal of the program time until opera as we know it today became a separate art.

In England the emotional and intellectual turmoil that both preceded and followed the Reformation stimulated playwrights to great activity, and England became the home of drama. This trend has continued to the present time so that translations of English plays have long been familiar to Continental audiences.

As the society around him provides the dramatist with his raw material, he must at least be a commentator if not a critic of society. Therefore, reactionary forces have always regarded him with some suspicion. Even the great Elizabethan playwrights had to be wary of offending the Queen, but Elizabeth kept on the right side of the line that divides strong government from tyranny. Her strength and the great length of her reign created a social stability that enabled all art to flourish—including the theatre. The uncertain political situation crested by her passing liberated the forces that were to destroy the monarchy. Among all members of the population, including the actors and the playwrights, there was a much diminished sense of allegiance to her successors.

It was not long before the playwrights again began to tilt at the ruling power—this time the State, not the Church. They were a corps of puny St. Georges who evoked low rumblings of protest from the tormented dragon.

It was not until the Commonwealth Government came into power in England that retaliation was serious. Seizing upon the Civil War as an excuse, the Lord Protector closed the playhouses in 1642 and outlawed the actors as rogues and vagabonds. These actions not only had a profound effect on the English theatre and the English playwright that has lasted up to the present day, but the psychological effect has become part of the actor's character.

The actor is not a revolutionary by temperament. He is a conservative in his dislike of any change that may affect his professional work. Because his profession is his whole life, he is likely to be steadfast and even obdurate in defending it. In the face of attack from without, the actors will always close their ranks. It was this characteristic which was to save the theatre during the Puritan Interregnum.

Determined to persist in their way of life, the people of the theatre formed themselves into a sort of underground movement after the closure of the playhouses. In spite of most formidable obstacles they staged illegal performances. Retribution swiftly followed. Soldiers raided the theatres, fined the members of the audience, destroyed the costumes, wrecked the auditoriums, and arrested the actors if they caught them. Those who were arrested were fined, whipped or imprisoned. Nevertheless, the actors who remained at liberty continued to act. Then they were deprived of all civil rights and their goods and possessions became forfeit to the State as were those of the Jews under the Nazi regime. Like the Jews, many were forced to flee the country; others joined the Royalist forces or went into hiding if unfitted to fight. Twenty years were to pass before the theatres were reopened.

It is interesting to surmise what would have happened to the theatre eventually if the Puritans had remained in power and England had continued as a Republic. Clues may be found in the kind of acting, but more particularly in the type of drama we have in the modern American theatre.

The Spaniards brought their theatre and some of their actors to South America and to many of the other American territories into which they infiltrated. Later on, with the settlement of the English in Virginia, there were minor offerings in the way of entertainment. These were provided by visiting English actors. On the whole, life was too unsettled—both during Colonial days and after the War of Independence—for the development of any of the arts. Later on, when the Northern States attracted numbers of emigrants, these pioneers had little leisure for entertainment. In any case most of them were Puritans and were as much opposed to dramatic entertainment as Oliver Cromwell had been.

However, the need for theatrical entertainment of some sort is a deep, primitive need. After a time what were known as "exhibition rooms" were opened. The diversions included edifying lectures and readings of a highly moralistic character. Eventually, readings from the works of Shakespeare were permitted. From this it was but a step to allowing his plays to be performed by visiting professional actors.

If Republicanism had continued in England it is most probable that theatres would gradually have reopened and that the plays of Shakespeare would have again been performed. There might also have been an increase in an innocuous form of entertainment known as a "masque," a medley of song, dance and recitation which had some popularity before the Lord Protector closed the theatres, and which he himself was reputed to have enjoyed. It is likely that the masque was the original inspiration of the musical comedy of a later age.

The Restoration turned drama in a very different direction from Puritanism. During his years on the continent of Europe Charles II saw a good deal of the court theatre of the period. On the whole, European playwrights had never reached the intellectual status of the English playwrights of the Elizabethan era, and the execution of Charles I had created much uneasiness in the minds of all European monarchs. Punishment would swiftly have overtaken any playwright who might have presented even the germ of a revolutionary idea. It was natural that with the restoration of the monarchy in England the new King was aware that Cromwell had been not altogether a fool in closing the theatres.

However, Charles II preferred the iron hand in the velvet glove to the mailed fist. Moreover he did not dislike the theatre; in fact, he loved it. So in order to foster the theatre on the one hand and keep a check on the activities of the playwrights on the other, he decreed that a small number of theatres might open under Royal Warrant. Two playhouses were permitted to open in London and the King further safeguarded his interests by granting the licenses to two men who had proved themselves ardent Royalists. These men could be relied upon to protect the interests of their royal patron and to safeguard their own by strongly opposing any move for the opening of other theatres. It mattered little to them that this policy betrayed and left destitute all but a tiny minority of the players who, having sacrificed all they possessed, risked liberty and even life itself to keep the theatre alive. With the passing of time more theatres did come into existence but it was really only after the death of Charles that the great period of "Restoration" theatre began.

State interference with man's intellectual curiosity or spiritual beliefs has produced many unexpected results, but none more curious than the aftereffects of the Puritan suppression of the theatre, followed by the monopoly of the reign of Charles II. But for this interference with and suppression of free theatre, Restoration drama might never have been what it was.

The people of the theatre—or rather the small number who could hope for employment after the restoration of the monarchy—fell into a savagely cynical mood when they found out what "liberation" meant. Gone was the dignity and poetry of the Elizabethan theatre, and the grandeur, tinged with a slightly gloomy philosophy, of the drama of the earlier Stuarts. Now serious drama would be suspect and the theatre had learned its lesson. This lesson has never since been forgotten. The British playwright has had his wings clipped. Even Bernard Shaw had to cover his socially critical plays with the sauce of satire to make them acceptable. In the theatre of the Restoration it was permissible to flick at society's foibles, but there must be no shadow of criticism to suggest that the new golden age might be of baser metal.

Elizabethan drama could be broad in expression, but it was written to appeal to all classes. Restoration drama was written to appeal to the tastes of a largely aristocratic audience with sophisticated tastes. The plays were the most licentious ever to be presented on the English stage. By the eighteenth century the most profligate theatre since the days of pagan Rome had been launched.

From its beginnings Restoration theatre had a new and powerful weapon. During his exile Charles II had become accustomed to actresses on the French stage. The female costumes of his reign, freed from the fetters of Puritanism, featured such a display of arms, shoulders and breasts that they sounded the knell of the boy actor. The actress heavily reinforced the old magic of the theatre with the most potent magic of all—sex appeal. Since the two monopoly theatres opened in London were the haunt of fashionable rakes and their hangers-on, there was much appreciation of this new appeal. The beginnings of striptease had been introduced.

That many of the first actresses were inspired to seek the stage out of a spirit of adventure rather than by any artistic impulse was scarcely surprising. The Puritans had destroyed the social as well as the artistic status of the profession and it was scarcely likely to attract women of sensibility or strict morality. At that time, any woman who earned her living was regarded as fair game, particularly a woman who displayed herself upon a public stage.

It is not remarkable that the playwrights of the period felt little allegiance to the society of the Restoration. While keeping on the right side of the King they seemed determined to flagellate all lesser men. Their plots concerned deception, greed, cuckoldry, lust and snobbery. But society had a thick skin and a perverse taste for this verbal flagellation.

Society was profligate; the recent outcasts of the theatre became just as profligate. Society was extravagant; the theatre would be more extravagant. Between the reopening of the theatres in 1660 and the final removal of the monopolies almost two hundred years later, the theatre came full circle in its fortunes. Its dying corpse was handed back to its rightful owners to do with as they would. The Restoration theatre had begun in a blaze of synthetic glory. At its best it was brilliant and amusing but it was also vulgar, dissipated, extravagant and brutally coarse. By the time the young Victoria ascended the throne the theatre was exhausted and in a state of collapse. Never had the people of the theatre been held in such disrepute and never had playwriting descended to such depths. It had become so feeble that many theatrical entertainments consisted of mixed programs of crude little farces or melo-dramas, with interludes of poor singing and inept dancing to fill out the bill.

It was at this period that more settled conditions, the creation of wealth and the growth of towns fostered the beginning of more extensive entertainments in the American states. The plays of Shakespeare were still popular but the plays of his successors, the playwrights of the Restoration, would have found little favor in a democratic society with puritanical ideals. Later on in the reign of Queen Victoria, however, English playwrights produced offerings which although poor in quality were irreproachable in moral tone. Audiences of the period, on both sides of the Atlantic, seemed to enjoy them.

By this time English actors, seeing in America the possibility of opportunities of a kind denied to them at home, where the theatre had not yet recovered its vitality, emigrated. Also there was a slow, spasmodic growth of a native American acting profession, although years were to pass before any of the actors were to attain international status. It was not until the days of Irving that the American star was to make much impact in London with the arrival of Edwin Booth.

Just as there was little to distinguish nineteenth-century American entertainment from that customary in England, so there was little in his aspect to distinguish the American actor from the English one. A long tradition had built up a style of acting in all Europe which the American actor naturally assimilated or at least tried to copy. The growth and emergence of the American actor as such took many years. Eventually he was to be helped in this process by a completely new form of entertainment, the films. Because of its nature and the rapid rate of its development, the new medium had to create its own players. The technique of film acting had limitations unknown to stage acting, but it also had advantages and opened up new vistas.

In an avid search for material with a strong visual appeal the films rapidly absorbed dramatic episodes in history ranging from Babylon to Rome and then to American history. The motion pictures also needed writers, far more than the theatre could supply even if the leading dramatists had been attracted to scenario writing. This medium, however, held little appeal for them. It was not until after the first World War that Hollywood became attractive to the playwright. At that time the work of the American playwright was still much like that of the English one. Plays by English authors were popular and many English companies came to perform them.

The status of the cinema was still far behind that of the theatre so it is scarcely surprising that it was some time before successful American writers and actors came to realize that they had anything to learn from the films. Once they did so they learned swiftly.

The early nineteen twenties saw the birth of a native American theatre. When the blazing star of the young Eugene O'Neill rose in the theatrical firmament the kind of actors and the style of acting needed for his plays were there. Simplicity, strength and vitality were the keynote of both the plays and the acting.

The plays of Eugene O'Neill offered great acting opportunities because here was a dramatist who drew his inspiration from two vital influences. These influences were the theatre of the Elizabethans and the drama of modern American society, a society deeply concerned with its own moral problems, many of which were rooted in its Puritan background. O'Neill himself, descended as he was from an Ulster family, was personally as much involved in this struggle as were the characters in his own plays.

The impact of plays of such stature and poetry was tremendous both at home and abroad. Here was a major playwright who seemed to be untouched by the historical influences of the European playwrights of the eighteenth century, the Restoration theatre of England or the banality and vulgarity prevalent in the French theatre of the nineteenth century.

It is scarcely an overstatement to say that the work of O'Neill and a number of American playwrights who have since become prominent has had a great influence on modern drama. Translations of the best American plays are very popular in Continental theatres and often enjoy a greater success than those by British playwrights.

Critics both in Great Britain and abroad often find new plays by English writers lacking in content and many British playwrights whose plays are a success on home ground owe a great debt to the British actor. The actor's understanding of his native scene often enables him to enrich and vitalize a play so that the audiences enjoy it far more than might otherwise be possible. When translations of such plays are staged abroad they may be far less successful.

In America, the actor is in a very different position to his English counterpart. He is less often confronted with the problem of making bricks without straw. He owes a tremendous debt to the best of the American playwrights.

The American actor has other problems of course, problems he shares with the English actor. Most of these are either economic or psychological.

CHAPTER two

THE ACTOR IN EMBRYO

The factors that shape the personality of the actor, as is the case with every individual, are to be found in his early environment. The emotions are always the dynamic, and reason the mechanism used, to progress toward the desired goal. Emotions are primitive impulses which have no relation to accepted moral codes. Because of this, the origin of the desire to attain success in any given field may be, in some degree, pathological. It should be remembered, however, that the origins of the pearl are also pathological since it is created out of the oyster's discomfort. Yet poets through the ages have sung the praise of the pearl while only Lewis Carroll has immortalized the oyster.

Like the pearl, the embryo actor comes into being through some psychic discomfort which forces him to reject the world accepted by the majority of people for a smaller world of painted canvas and artificial light in which individuals speak not their own words but the words of others and act out interpretations of passions not their own.

This acting gives great riches to the world. It is, and has been for several centuries, the most potent of all arts in the Western world—an art for which its artists make great sacrifices and gain comparatively meager material reward.

What have they in common, these men and women who have as their goal the world of fantasy to be found on the other side of the stage curtains?

Emotionally the actor is, in many ways, what a psychologist might call an immature personality. That is, he continues to follow patterns of behavior generally abandoned by others throughout the gradual stages of their journey into maturity.

Babies develop awareness of their environment long before they can speak and their first responses to this environment are often imitations of the actions of older children, parents or other adults. All children are actors and must be if they are to develop. Their home is their theatre and their parents the first directors. The child's first roles are dictated by parental wisdom or parental prejudices.

One of the very first things a baby comes to realize is that crying attracts attention. Subnormal babies cry less than normal ones because they do not grasp the correlation between crying and attention from others. The more intelligent and observant the child the less likely he is to be a quiet baby. As with the actor, the baby's "bits of business" are never aimless but always purposeful.

After realizing that crying brings results, there is the discovery that a smile can be devastatingly effective. So charm, one of the most potent psychological weapons, is born.

While writing this book I have had a daily opportunity of watching a masterly performance put on every morning by a baby who lives across the street.

This baby is put out in his perambulator on the sidewalk, with a number of toys to amuse him.

When he was too young to move about very much, he howled when he got bored. As time passed, he was able to move about. He accidentally knocked a toy out onto the pavement and a passer-by immediately stopped, picked it up and talked to the child. After a few days the baby developed into a real actor. He would peer cautiously around in all directions and then, when a passer-by hove in sight, pick up a toy and drop it overboard. Naturally the passer-by noticed the toy, picked it up and restored it to the child. The time in his pram was no longer a bore but a most exciting interlude.

As the toys were thrown out so frequently, correct timing became difficult. The baby got flustered because of the speed necessary to attract and then dispose of one good Samaritan before the next one arrived on the scene. Pedestrians began to spot the fact that the toys were being flung out purposely and did not stop. The expression of frustration and anger on the baby's face as he leaned out of his perambulator to shout inarticulate abuse at those who passed without stopping was like that of a busker ignored by a theatre queue. It was this baby's first realization that those who seemed to exist solely to minister to him had lives and interests of their own, and also critical faculties. He was not and could not always be the center of uncritical attention. That is the first unwelcome lesson that every infant must learn.

Then begins the struggle that preoccupies every one of us, in some degree, for the rest of our lives. The struggle between our desires as individuals and the attitude of others toward those desires. The individual is constantly torn between satisfying his own desires and conforming to social demands in order to be accepted as a member of a group.

At first the infant makes every effort to retain his privileged place. Howls, smiles, chatter or even sheer naughtiness are among the devices used. Usually, under external pressure and because of increasing interests in the external world, the infant abdicates his throne. However, some individuals do not do so.

There are various reasons why the inner world, where the child is the center of attention, may remain more attractive than the outer one. The infant may have been specially cosseted because he was not robust at birth, or was the victim of a number of illnesses. He may be an only child or an eldest child whose siblings were not born until some years had elapsed. He may be a youngest child, or a son in a family of girls. He may simply be an unusually pretty child. The mother may have transferred an undue amount of emotion to her child, perhaps as a result of becoming a widow or a grass widow, or even through disappointments in her relationship with her husband.

The longer the child is the center of attention at home the more aware he is of the contrast between his place in the home and his much less important position outside it. Two courses are open to him. He may cling to his place in the home and become a spoiled darling while remaining a nonentity in the outer world, or he may use his intelligence to try and attract as much attention and favor in the larger world as he enjoys at home. If he takes the latter course he may ultimately become an actor. Actors cannot be taught to *act* in drama schools, although they can be taught a great deal which enables them to improve their art. Practically every student of drama has been acting since childhood, as indeed every social being does to a greater or lesser degree. In the professional theatre there are good, proficient and even bad actors. In the world outside the theatre there are thousands of bad actors and a few good ones.

The child who fights for a place in the world soon realizes that speech is a splendid medium for attracting attention. Many children become indefatigable talkers because they discover talking to be an activity which cannot easily be ignored. The embryo actor is usually a voluble child and never loses that trait. Actors love speech. They willingly undertake the labor of learning lines for the sheer pleasure of assimilating and regurgitating them.

The child who fights for and retains privilege is soon aware of the difference between himself and lesser mortals. He begins to feel a little guilty and wishes to prove worthy of the favor he enjoys. Atonement usually takes a form which both repays favors shown and at the same time keeps the favored one in the center of the stage.

In his autobiography Noël Coward mentions several episodes of this kind. One concerns an early foray into the outer world when he was taken to church for the first time. Hearing the organ, he danced up the aisle because he felt this was the least he could do when music was being played for him. A friend of mine, who later developed into a singer and an actor, sang loudly when taken to church and attracted so much attention that his embarrassed mother removed him. These are good examples of atonement which assuages guilt feelings and also centers attention on the individual. Guilt feelings always have been most readily assuaged and sublimated in religious services. Many actors have, in adolescence, toyed with the notion of becoming men of the church. Some have done so. One of the former was the late Douglas Fairbanks. Fortunately a discerning and kindly clergyman managed to divert the young Fairbanks' missionary zeal into more suitable chan-

nels. Clergymen are often interested in amateur theatri-
cals. One remarked to a professional actor, "I have often
thought I should like to have gone on the stage but I have
the advantage over you actors. I always give a solo performance."

The child who refuses to give up the small kingdom in
which he rules finds, as he passes from childhood to adolescence, that he is driven from one terrain to another as
the demands of the external world encroach upon him.
Given ammunition of the right kind—that is, intelligence,
imagination and creative ability—he may gain entrance to
a stronghold which he can occupy indefinitely. That
stronghold is the theatre.

Usually it is during adolescence that most potential
actors begin to think of a stage career. It is at this time
that the conflict between their own desires and the demands of the society in which they are expected to take
their place becomes acute. No one is more susceptible to
the magic of the theatre than the stage-struck adolescent
who has no experience of it. To the child of theatrical
parents, sets are but painted flats and players people who,
in private life, may display a kind of petty jealousy that
would be condemned in boarding school. My own child
was most upset the first time she saw a favorite adopted
uncle die at the end of *The Two Mrs. Carrolls,* but she
never entirely forgave him when he rose to his feet and
dusted off his trouser legs. She felt she had been deceived.

Few students of drama have had any childhood acquaint-
ance with the backstage of the theatre. Adolescents who
have, the child players, do not generally desire to return
to the theatre in later life. Among those who do, fewer
still rise to stardom.

When hopeful adolescents consult me about their
chances of "going on the stage," the questions I ask often

seem to them irrelevant to the great problem on hand. I start out by mentioning that a theatrical career is precarious. But everyone knows that now. The aspiring actor replies that if a person has real talent he must succeed. I say that the stage is hard work. The answer to that is that the aspirant is prepared to work hard. The dialogue then proceeds along the following lines, with "A" for aspirant and "M" for me:

M. Do you wish to enter a drama school?
A. Do you think that is really necessary? Couldn't I get some sort of job in repertory and learn that way?
M. What do you think you could do in repertory at present?
A. I don't quite know but I'm sure I could make myself useful. Anyhow, don't some repertory companies take you if you pay something?
M. Some do. But a busy producer has no time to teach anyone. In any case you must know how to speak and move before you can get on with the business of learning to act—or rather of learning the technique of acting.
A. I see. Suppose I am willing to go to a drama school. How do I set about it?
M. You read plays and learn excerpts from them and then you apply for an audition. If you pass it and are able to pay the fees you become a student.
A. Oh, I thought you just paid and got in. How much are the fees?

The aspirant is then usually extremely surprised at the costs. I mention scholarships, but the amount of work involved sounds too formidable. Then I may be asked about training in evening classes. Once it is clear that the work will be just as hard, and may be spread over a longer period, this alternative loses its attractions.

One can usually tell the young people who will face up

to the hard study and the subsequent hardships of a stage career. Some do win scholarships, and others do go through a full course of training in evening classes.

There are many reasons why the life of a successful player appears so satisfactory to the adolescent, and to a certain type of socially unreconciled individual. The famous actor is the kingpin of a group whose reason for existence seems to be to revolve around him. Social and personal problems are solved, as well as economic ones, because the theatrical profession is not just an occupation. It is a way of life. The stage caters to many emotional needs; and it is not the small stage of early domestic environment with its limited audience but a much larger one, divided only by a curtain from vast audiences. Curtain up, and there is the unique opportunity of capturing the attention of a mass of people and obtaining enormous approval and thunderous applause. Applause satisfies that all-consuming appetite for love, praise and personal power which is so immoderate in the primitive being, the small child and the actor.

Most actors are not primarily concerned with securing money or property and many of them have a strong sense of dedication to their profession. I once saw a young actor, who had been unemployed for some time, collapse from hunger during a rehearsal. I have also known hard-up actors to go without food in order to pay for a ticket to a play they wanted to see. Destitution may force an actor into seeking a temporary job in some other occupation, but as a rule he will leave it as soon as he has saved a few pounds to keep him going while he seeks another stage engagement. He will do this not once but many times over. It is emotion, not reason, that is the driving force behind these struggles to remain in the theatre at all costs. For not all such doughty fighters are potential stars. Many are mediocre, or even bad, actors.

In the shockingly overcrowded state of the profession today a fanatical attachment to his art is necessary to enable even a competent actor to stay the course. Those who do not have a strong sense of dedication gradually weaken and leave the stage.

According to the records compiled by Equity, the British actors' trade union, although about sixteen hundred new members join in a year, the total membership figures remain about the same. Even when allowance is made for the tolls taken by old age, retirement and death, it is obvious that a large number of actors drop out of the fight. A considerable number of young women get little or no work after leaving drama school and then marry. Behind these figures of some sixteen hundred new memberships annually, and approximately sixteen hundred memberships which are not renewed, is a dismal picture of thwarted individuals destined to frustrated lives in occupations that bring them no real satisfaction.

In Britain, this is a modern problem for which the too numerous drama schools, mostly in London, are responsible. In the days when training could only be obtained in the theatre, after lessons had been taken in elocution and dancing, employment was automatically regulated. No theatre would take in more people than it could use. It was a rough-and-ready method. The argument against it is that much talent may have been lost to the theatre. Perhaps this was so. Yet many stage-struck young people were saved the humiliating experience of spending two or three years in a drama school, followed by anything up to four or five years trying to gain a foothold in the theatre, and then failing utterly.

It is also true, of course, that many students do not

complete the two years' course. At six-month intervals most British schools of acting weed out those who are not making satisfactory progress. There are many reasons for rejection, but too often a student fails because of psychological characteristics which could have been brought to light by adequate testing before the school accepted him. The true reason for such a rejection is often not given. To do so would involve the school in an awkward situation. A girl who cuts lessons for social engagements or who goes to too many late parties, and is too tired to concentrate, can easily be told why she is unlikely to make good. It is less easy with one who, though she may have potential talent, is an embryo nymphomaniac who will therefore disrupt social and professional relationships and sow discord wherever she goes.

The kind of entrance examination that the would-be student undergoes is far too superficial to reveal many of the psychological complexities which must inevitably lead to failure. I have known students with manic-depressive temperaments who were as unamenable to discipline in the elated phase of exhibitionism and aggression as in the depressed phase of deep despair. Only very detailed psychological testing would have brought such a handicap to light *before* the student started work in the school. I have also known students who have been thrown out of drama schools for reasons which must have been just as apparent before they were ever accepted—that they were too tall or too small. One student had to be rejected because his appearance was so vulgar that even when he played serious dramatic roles the audience was inclined to titter.

As every drama school is, to a greater or lesser degree, influenced by financial considerations, it is not surprising that there are always more students of acting than the profession will be able to absorb. Nor is it surprising that perhaps 90 per cent of the students have been impelled to seek a career in acting for reasons which are unlikely to lead them to success. It is inevitable that adolescents should lack a deep understanding of themselves—but that is all the more reason why they should not be fed into a machine which ignores their individual psychological natures and then, after a bewildering period of trial and error, spews out a large porportion as unassimilative material.

Too many of these schools are run on this conveyer-belt system. They demand blind obedience and the student has to conform to the pattern or get out. And what is this pattern? On the whole, it is a pattern that met the needs of the actor of sixty years ago about the time when the Royal Academy of Dramatic Art was founded. Actors at that period often gave splendid performances that met the demands of the plays in which they performed and won large audiences as well. But neither the plays nor the performances would suit the audiences of today. Yet the same rigid training prevails and has remained largely uninfluenced by modern theatrical developments.

This training often has an adverse effect on sensitive students but a student's ability to "stand up" to the discipline is regarded as a test of his suitability for the profession. American students training over here often find the traditional atmosphere irksome and frustrating and may not always complete the course. The same is true of a number of British students.

It is true that some of the schools are not entirely unaware of how psychological factors that may affect a student can hamper his progress. Several schools do make arrangements for a disturbed student to consult a psychiatrist. The fact remains however that if psychological testing were undertaken before students entered a drama school, much unhappiness and tragedy might be prevented. If such testing were customary it would not necessarily mean that all students who had special psychic problems or who were oversensitive would be debarred from entering, it would simply mean that the teachers would have more knowledge of their students as individuals and would be better able to help them. A number of students do leave owing to breakdowns, and attempted suicides during the school years or immediately afterwards are not at all uncommon.

American drama schools are not so encumbered by old traditions as is the case in England, although the present cult of Stanislavsky's early method could become as rigorous in its way as traditional English methods are in their way. Toward the end of his life Stanislavsky deprecated too complete an adherence to his original theories of acting. Certainly learning by "the method" can impose great psychological stress on students.

However, theories and traditions are seldom without some virtue. The virtue of the English tradition is that students emerge from school well equipped in voice and movement for the performance of classical plays, and particularly for performances of Shakespeare's plays. This is no longer so in the United States, where there seems to be lack of training to equip students for such parts. As in the nineteenth century, the most popular performances of Shakespeare appear to be those given by visiting English companies. This is regrettable when it is remembered that the Hamlet of John Barrymore at the Haymarket Theatre in London in 1926 is still remembered both by critics and public alike as either the greatest Hamlet they had ever seen or one of the three best within living memory.

I am sure there are potential Shakespearean stars of

international quality among young actors in the United States today and that only the right training in speech technique and physical plasticity is needed to bring these potentialities to fruition.

CHAPTER three

THROUGH THE LOOKING
GLASS

Because of the difference between the actor's basic emotional pattern and that of the non-actor, the actor becomes conscious of his separateness from society early in his life. His awareness of this psychological chasm may first arise when he timidly voices his desire for a theatrical career. Many parents of would-be actors have discussed with me the question of acting as a career, though to use the word "discussion" (in this connection) is scarcely accurate. One cannot reasonably discuss views based on blind emotional prejudice. These prejudices fall under two headings—those relating to morals and those relating to economics; there is a point, however, where the two become linked. Many people feel that if an individual wants to earn his living doing something that gives him great pleasure, something he enjoys, this in itself smacks of immorality. So-called realists have often told me that because actors and writers get such satisfaction out of their work they should not expect any great material reward.

Ours is an aggressive society which can be violent and punitive in its reactions to disobedience or nonconformity, yet benign when its demands are met. The foundations of such a society are based upon conquest and material gain. The young male is expected to choose an occupation in which he can reap material rewards as soon as possible so that he (and his parents) can bask in the approval of their particular social group.

In Great Britain another influence also prevails when a young man chooses his career, that of tradition. I knew a young medical student whose family had had at least one physician in each generation in an unbroken line back to the time of Charles II. There are upper middle-class families whose members have figured in politics since the days of the first Queen Elizabeth. There are more humble families who have adhered to certain crafts, trades or occupations for many generations. There are also of course a few families who have been associated with the theatre for a century or more. They are in a tiny minority. Very often the young man who wishes to become an actor finds family opposition to his desire all the stronger because he is expected to follow his father's footsteps when it comes to earning a living.

Concerning this, one significant fact emerged from my survey, from conversations with actors and from a study of the lives of famous actors. In a large number of cases the actor comes from a home where the father has not played a dominating role or has been absent for long periods. Free from pressure to emulate the father, the desire to create, nascent in some form or other in nearly all small children, may develop strongly in adolescence.

Once embarked on his career the actor finds that many

things connected with it set him apart from society as he knew it. There is the fact that he may have to leave home in order to train or obtain employment, so he loses touch with relatives and friends. Even if he lives in a large city where he can be trained and also get work, his working hours cut him off from the social life he has known. In addition to all this the economics of his profession also create social difficulties. For instance, a young actor may also earn about £6 a week (less than 20 dollars) when he is employed and he is certain to have long periods of unemployment. In the United States, Actors' Equity has recently negotiated a new minimum wage of 45 dollars a week. This is only two dollars more than an unemployed man with a wife and two children gets from his welfare check. For this reason a struggling actor cannot participate in very much social life.

There is one difference between society in the United States and in Great Britain that may help the American actor to feel that poverty and periods of unemployment do not mark him off from his fellows, and that is that a great many young American men expose themselves to financial hazards in their early lives. In a small country like England there is now little scope for such adventurous souls, so they either emigrate or settle for security at home instead.

Yet in both the United States and Great Britain the actor is set apart from the mass of the community in one very significant way. Although he meets the same obligations and pays the same taxes as other citizens, his situation is different from theirs when he is unemployed. No employment agency has the machinery to find the out-of-work actor an engagement. The nearest they get is to put him in touch with a large store that wants a Santa Claus for the Christmas period. As a stopgap the actor may accept other employment. Often it is unskilled and not well paid and he has greater difficulty than ever in seeking an engagement in a theatre. Naturally he tries to get such an engagement as soon as possible and leaves his job. As a result, the actor now has a reputation for unreliability in the labor market. Yet in view of the difficulties of his situation he has ample excuse for his seeming defection.

While it is true that many of the actor's economic difficulties are due to the overcrowding in his profession, it is also true that the actor has found that loyalty to anything but his art is unrewarding. Therefore he is prejudiced against bureaucracy in all its forms. Since only concerted action and willingness to yield a certain amount of power to his union can improve his lot, amelioration of his vicissitudes is slow and difficult. British Equity has had at least as much difficulty in persuading its members to accept rules and discipline in order to improve the position of the profession as a whole, as it has had in trying to get theatrical employers to accept such demands as have been made upon them. Not only do many members of the profession accept contracts or engagements under terms that have been interdicted by their union, but they are often unaware that Equity has rulings in such matters.

Here again tradition plays some part in the actor's total attitude to union rules. England had a long history of industrialization behind her before a trade-union movement arose. Trade unionism was something for the masses. White-collar workers did not welcome its intrusion into their lives, because they either belonged to the middle classes or aspired to do so. In the United States the rise of industry coincided with the rise of trade unions in Great Britain and other European countries, so that even among professional workers there was less opposition to unions or associations of some kind. Also, paradoxically enough, the intense commercialism of the American theatrical scene has favored trade unionism. For one thing, it wiped out the actor-managers, a number of whom still exist in the English provincial theatres and who are, on the whole, very reactionary, since they are not only fighting for the survival of their own theatres or companies as business propositions but for their own existence in the profession. When forced to seek employment in the open market they are often found playing small parts at poor salaries in second-rate theatres.

In most of the replies to my questionnaire where such matters as the personal economics of the actor were touched upon it was evident that the actor had little or no awareness of his economic situation, nor of the relationship between his particular economic problems and the economic forces that underlie the economic structure. Most of them were convinced that they only needed the legendary "break" to find indefinite security as well as success artistically. This is not strange in a field where there are so many examples of apparent failure being turned to success. There are many actors who have been destitute and hungry, and then suddenly had an engagement that led to prosperity. It is not surprising that actors attribute so much to luck and have so little understanding of the influences that shape our economics, and hence so little political consciousness.

The apathy that many actors feel toward Equity is not therefore remarkable, particularly when it is remembered that an actor is an intense individualist. That is yet another reason why he finds it difficult to delegate very much power to his own trade union.

Both in my survey and the history of the industry there are indications that the film actor often regards himself as more progressive-minded and practical than the stage actor. He is not a traditionalist and may even have revolutionary inclinations. One film actor expressed a view held by many, which is that an actor should have political awareness and that through his art he should help to mold the social pattern as well as reflect it.

If an actor does have any interest in politics and economics or even very much social awareness, he is more likely to gravitate toward the film studio than the theatre. The inveterate stage actor still regards the film industry as a wealthy Philistine uncle whose patronage is financially valuable but culturally worthless.

The stage actor who is out of work may be discontented with social conditions but usually remains uninterested in their causes. Among British actors there is one explanation for this which does not as yet apply to the actor in the United States. In very many instances the British actor has gone straight from school to drama school. This is partly due to the fact that he can compete for a scholarship to a drama school at the age of eighteen and, if his parents cannot or will not make him an allowance for maintenance, his local education authority will usually do so after he has won a scholarship. In other cases the parents are prepared to pay all expenses and all the aspirant has to do is to pass the entrance examination to the school.

For some years past I have advocated that the would-be actor should spend from two to three years earning a living after he leaves school and before he becomes a drama student. One well-known London drama school is now inclined to recommend this system also.

Yet there are psychological reasons why the actor is likely to remain rather uninterested in politics or economics. First of all, he harbors little aggression toward social conditions when these are unfavorable. The very nature of his occupation affords him ample opportunity to play out fantasies and get rid of aggressions in the world of the imagination which is his heritage. Also, he has the yearning of the child to be loved and accepted, and society does not love its social critics nor accept its social rebels.

It has been said that the modern English actor has such a strong desire to be identified with the socially accepted members of society that he is becoming too refined to be able to portray characters outside his adopted class environment. Critics find far more realism in the character acting of French or American actors in the proletarian roles. There may be some truth in this criticism. It must be remembered, however, that neither in France nor in America were the actors ever deprived of civil rights and classed by the State as rogues and vagabonds.

The punishment inflicted on his forebears is part of the psychological heritage of the English professional actor. His attempt to conform, to become indistinguishable from the mass of conventional good citizens, is in part an effort to obtain a reversal of the verdict which the State and society passed upon his predecessors. Press agents are often bedeviled by the dilemma of exploiting a star's personality—although there may be little that is suitable for exploitation—or deliberately creating colorful incidents that may misfire and antagonize the public.

While the majority of young actors have little aggression against society, naturally many aspects of theatrical work make it attractive to the kind of person that Freud called the "social discontent," or, in the more common vernacular, a social misfit. Such people often have daydreams of personal glory easily won, but they usually lack the self-discipline necessary to attain this glory even if they have the necessary talent. They seldom achieve real stardom and, when they do, almost always fail to retain it.

This is because the social misfit lacks real strength of

character as a rule. He has not the ability to change his own character or overcome obstacles in his environment which, with persistence, he might overcome. Nor can he accept what cannot be changed in the outer world or in the present-day theatre. So he may drift from one type of employment in entertainment to another, without successfully adapting himself to any of them.

The actor who has always had one goal in sight—that is, to act—may have less intellect than many social misfits who are attracted to the theatrical profession. He may have so little intellect that he cannot even see his own limitations. I remember an old actor, who had little ability and had never played a really important part in his life, who said that if only producers would let him go on the stage and be himself he would certainly be a success. Yet as long as he could obtain small parts he did remain in the theatre until he retired at quite a late age. He accepted what he could not change. The more intelligent social misfit would never be able to do this.

The sense of insecurity that the actor does feel, seldom springs from doubts about his own abilities. He suffers the insecurity of the child who must always have love and approval to sustain him. For this reason even a star cannot feel really secure. When he has the prize of a run-of-the-play contract in the West End or on Broadway he still has no real security, even economically. The play may be withdrawn after a tryout. Even if it gets into town it may be a flop. In engagements outside capital cities other disasters may befall. Each disaster brings a sense of public rebuff but not any suspicion of personal failure.

The refusal to accept personal failure as being the result of professional inadequacy is easier in the theatre than in any other profession. It is only in the theatre that an individual may still consider himself an active participant even if he only works for a few weeks or months in any one year.

It is not remarkable that in such circumstances an actor may have little perception of the gulf between his abilities and his wishes. One is reminded of stars who have suffered resounding failure in roles for which they were completely unfitted in every way, including age and physical appearance. These errors of judgment can only be the result of an utterly unrealistic conception of themselves. In many cases there is an unhappy synthesis between deprivation and desire. The clown wishes to play Hamlet, the sexually impotent to portray a great lover, the timid to enact formidable characters, the actress whose face is not perfect, whose figure was never her fortune, to take the stage as Cleopatra.

Nevertheless these kinds of failure are readily enough cast into oblivion. Actors seldom commit suicide as a result of failure or of prolonged unemployment. The suicide rate among them is relatively small, and their suicides are usually due to fear of some approaching scandal or are the result of some emotional entanglement. The deep sense of failure and worthlessness which is the usual cause of suicide among non-actors does not afflict the people of the theatre. Such a neurosis differs in pattern from the neurosis generally prevalent among the acting profession.

CHAPTER four

THE ACTOR'S SEX PROBLEMS

Most non-actors have a very definite and uniform picture of the psychology of the actor. Many of them are extremely dogmatic and almost all agree on two related points. The first is that the good actor should really feel all the emotions he portrays while he plays them. If he does not he must be insincere. Secondly, if he is not truly feeling the emotions of the characters he portrays, he must also be insincere in his own emotions. This is a very interesting example of deduction from a mistaken premise. Everyone connected with the theatre is so accustomed to hearing these two related statements that they seldom bother to argue about them. Together they create one of the greatest barriers between the actor and his fellow human beings.

No one accused Pavlov's dogs and rats of "insincerity" when he had conditioned them to react automatically to certain noises associated with their feeding after the food had been removed. Emotions are the food of the actor. When he studies and rehearses a part he is stimulated to a certain pattern of emotional reactions. Gradually these responses become automatic but they were originally spontaneous.

Responses to a given stimulus must become automatic after a time, but that does not make such responses any the less sincere. Any non-actor can prove this point very easily. The audience is part of a play; a play would not be a play without an audience, since it is the actor's business to make the audience feel. If a member of the audience goes for several nights in a row to a play which has moved him deeply, he may be just as deeply impressed on the last night, but familiarity will cause him to react in a slightly different way with each performance. The actor, however, has to see to it that *he* does not behave differently at each performance. If he did, the result would be just as disastrous to the whole play as if the interlocking pieces in a jigsaw puzzle were subtly to change their shapes. It is the actor's business to act—not merely to react. He can act—that is, he can give a performance which varies very little—night after night but his inner reactions while performing may differ a great deal.

One of the director's greatest problems is to see that the cast keeps the quality of its acting at the level he set at the beginning of the production. When the actors let down, the play begins to disintegrate.

The falsity of the layman's premise that the actor must be insincere in his responses to real-life situations is obvious. In real life, unlike the drama, situations never repeat themselves exactly. It is true that to the spectator they may appear to do so, but the participants in a real-life situation are dealing with subjective as well as objective realities. The quarrels of two lovers may seem to be boringly repetitive to their immediate circle, but to the protagonists each battle has as many subtle differences as any campaign in a major war.

It may be true, and often is, that an actor's love affairs and friendships are stormy and varied. This is not due to insincerity but rather to the reverse. Disasters are caused by the actor's trigger-swift reactions in emotionally charged situations. Insincerity on the other hand very often has its roots in coolly calculated reasoning.

The layman who accuses the actor of insincerity is probably confused by the actor's ability to be all things to all men on certain levels. He forgets that, as emotions are the actor's stock-in-trade, the actor is far more aware of other people's emotions than is the average layman. The actor is extremely conscious of what is expected of him in the way of response, and, so long as deep emotions are not involved, he reacts accordingly. Deep emotions are only involved when the actor's personal world is threatened. For instance, praise of the work of one actor to another is almost certain to provoke an inordinate display of resentment.

Why is professional jealousy so virulent in the acting profession? It is because, unlike any other artist, the actor puts into his work the whole of himself and everything he is. Any other kind of artist is at least at one remove from that perilous position. The physical appearance of a writer or a painter will not seriously affect criticism of his work. When the actor is criticized, or a rival player praised, it is a very different matter.

However mature an actor may be in years and in art, his unconscious emotions are still those of the child who wishes to remain a monarch. If this were not so he would no longer be an actor. This does not mean that the actor cannot be emotionally mature at other levels. He is an artist not a monster.

Insofar as the actor's personal emotional life, that is his sex life, differs from that of other citizens, the explanation is to be found at much deeper levels than the superficial one of conscious insincerity.

A well-known psychiatrist with whom I discussed the actor's sex psychology believed that many men turn to the stage because there they can enact roles of far greater sex potency than they could fulfill in real life. There is probably some truth in this.

It must be remembered that sexual potency is not a purely physical attribute like height or weight. If this were so, impotence would not be amenable to psychological treatment. The actor, together with the priest, has the greatest opportunities of sublimating his sexual emotions. At the other end of the scale, the laborer at a mechanical job has the least. In any event sexual inadequacy—except of a purely physical kind—is not the cause, but the result of neurosis.

Insofar as the actor may be accused of inconstancy in his human relationships—which is what his critics mean when they say he is insincere—the reasons are manifold. They are to be found in the actor's psychological make-up and in his social history.

The actor starts off as a child who is not willing to give up privileges. In order to retain the favored position he gains, everything connected with his profession must come first. He is a dedicated man. It is true that some actors who leave the profession state that they have "given up the stage for marriage," but no *successful* actor gives up the stage in order to get married; there is no reason why he should do so. But the explanation helps to salve the deep hurt the unsuccessful actor suffers. It also wins public approval, for the public still secretly regards the actor as a cunning fellow who contracts out of civic responsibilities.

The marriages of those who remain in the profession are subject to greater strain than those of less sensitive individuals than actors. It is not possible for someone whose occupation demands hypersensitivity to leave that trait behind him when he steps outside the stage door. Then, too, there is the social attitude to stage divorces. Because of its lingering belief that the stage is immoral, society does not expect the same behavior in marital relations from the actor as it does from other sections of the community. This is so despite the fact that if the actor commits misdemeanors of other kinds severe punishment is often meted out. But the actor suffers neither professional eclipse nor social disapproval if his marriage is dissolved.

On the material plane divorce causes less upheaval to the actor than to more settled members of the community who remain in one place and probably in one dwelling for the greater part of their lives. No actor could do this, the nature of his employment makes changes inevitable.

Furthermore, the actor is exposed to much more temptation to philander than are many other members of the community. Fan idolatry is only the more obvious aspect of the attraction members of the theatrical profession have for a large section of the public. The actor knows from experience that women often expect and indeed desire him to behave toward them in a way contrary to the prevailing sexual code. Although they ostensibly support this code, they may be angry and resentful if the actor does so. The actress also is only too familiar with sexual advances based on the social attitude to the profession. There is still a fairly widespread belief that an actress, if not actually promiscuous, must be at least sexually amoral.

The problem of the businessman married to his work rather than to his wife has provided the plots for dozens of plays and novels. Yet the stage player is more irrevocably wedded to his profession than any other member of the community. Stage folk have less time, opportunity or energy to devote to their domestic lives than almost any other group. It is inevitable that many marriages break up.

Nevertheless the actor is not a social rebel: consciously or unconsciously he longs for social approval, longs to be part of society. Comparative statistics of the percentage of divorces among stage players and among other groups might well yield surprising results. When the Joneses of Acacia Avenue get a divorce it is not news, but when two stars do so, it is reported on the front pages, and a divorce among any members of the theatrical profession is almost certain to get some mention in the press.

Marriages are not just sexual partnerships, they are also social contracts. It is probable that it is in the social rather than the sexual field that many theatrical marriages come to grief. The layman who marries a professional actress finds that her hours of work completely disrupt the program of living to which he is accustomed. Also he is likely to be known as "Miss So-and-So's husband." These are sources of discomfort and discontent. The girl who marries an actor usually finds that unless she is prepared to dedicate her life to her husband's profession, and enjoys doing so, she is living in a vacuum.

When an actress and actor marry, the marriage is likely to be much more successful provided the pair can cope with the terrible dragon of professional jealousy. So long as their careers remain at the same level this may be reasonably easy, but when one partner begins to enjoy greater success than the other the marriage has much less chance of success, particularly when it is the woman who forges ahead.

It is easy to suggest that it would be better if stage players did not marry—but scarcely practicable since they desire social love and approval and are not of the stuff of which rebels are made. The more the actor defies society the more his behavior resembles that of an angry and resentful small boy sticking out his tongue at grownups. By his very nature he is incapable of the austere dignity of the social pioneer putting his iconoclastic beliefs into practice.

How does the stage player's occupational skill in love-making affect his reactions in real life? That is another question put by the layman. No more than the accepted social code of behavior in any group. An actor's emotional reactions toward a love object are not weakened because he has a more facile approach than the non-actor. Stage love scenes invoke none of the emotions invoked by those off-stage. If they do they are failures as love scenes. The most successful stage lovers are married couples of fairly long standing, because they have least self-consciousness and can continue to play their love scenes expertly even when their private relationship may be very unsuccessful.

Another proof that genuine sexual response is little affected by stage love-making is to be found in the fact that many of the most famous lovers of the musical stage, or in all but the most demanding of dramas, are not normal males but homosexuals. Of this, of course, audiences are as a whole unaware.

The normally sexed young actor is usually keenly conscious of the dilemma in which he finds himself regarding his enjoyment of an adult emotional life. Here are the opinions of two players whose points of view are typical of many in the same position:

I don't see how I can hope to marry. To begin with, unless I become an established success I could not support a family. Even if I were a success I think my wife would have a pretty thin time because, as far as I am concerned, I know my work would always come first. I would like to have a love affair with someone of whom I was fond and who was genuinely fond of me. Yet I move about so much that such a thing simply isn't possible. Perhaps I shall have to be content with casual affairs but so far, even though I am conscious that I am not living a normal life, I don't want those.

The other is a more sophisticated young man:

I have had a number of casual affairs. It isn't difficult because so many girls seem to think it is wonderful to have a romance with an actor. Girls in the theatre are different of course. If they do have an affair they usually make it so clear that their feelings aren't seriously involved that I get browned off. The whole thing begins to seem sordid. But what's the alternative? I can't afford to marry and I'm not sure I want to anyhow. A young actor has to be free.

These views are probably held by hundreds of young actors, but, since emotion and not reason is the dynamic in a sex relationship, many young actors do marry and many of the marriages are wrecked because of the conflicting demands of a theatrical career and of a successful marriage partnership.

To some extent the problem is less difficult for the young actress. At least she is not made to accept economic responsibilities as the price of marriage. It is true that in her early days it is unlikely that she will be able to marry within the profession, since young actors simply cannot afford to marry. She is likely, of course, to get many favorable opportunities through meeting well-to-do non-actors to marry outside the profession. But that may mean giving up professional acting.

By the time she has established herself in the profession it is very likely that she will have married an actor who has also gained a modicum of success. Marriage either inside or outside the profession is the general rule then.

The attitude of the actress toward sex morality or behavior is no more uniform than that of women outside the theatre. The actress with little talent and amoral tendencies is naturally inclined to use sex appeal to bolster up her chances of success. The actress who is fanatically dedicated to her career is unlikely to want the responsibilities of a home and a possible family in her early youth. Both these types may prefer temporary to permanent relationships.

Yet temporary relationships are not as common now as they were in the past. Here is what an old actor had to say of the English theatre of thirty years ago:

When I first went into the theatre it was quite usual for a leading lady to arrive at first rehearsal, have a look at the male members of the Company and earmark the most attractive. She would probably have an affair with him for the run of the play or tour. If he was a less experienced player than she was herself she would help him with his work and give him a lot of useful tips. Others in the Company would have affairs too. This may sound idyllic but it wasn't really. There was a lot of unhappiness as well as happiness. Now of course everything is different because of more intense competition and also because there are so many men in the theatre who aren't interested in women.

One reason why actresses are so moral as far as men in the company are concerned is that it is rare to find a company in which there are not a number of homosexuals. In many companies it would be difficult for a woman to find a lover even if she wanted to.

CHAPTER five

HOMOSEXUALITY AND THE
THEATRE

Because there are many men in the theatre who are not interested in women it is sometimes assumed that there is some common factor between homosexuality and the ability to act. The explanation is not that all actors have homosexual tendencies but that theatrical life has a strong attraction for the homosexual.

The reasons for this are obvious. The stage offers an opportunity for the homosexual to obtain power and authority which he would fear to fight for in real life. He can, as far as his audiences are concerned, appear to be a potent and fascinating lover in romantic roles which his immature emotional development would prevent his undertaking in the outside world. Also he is in an environment where a love of fantasy, and a delight in dressing up, is approved.

It is only during the past thirty years that the homo-

56

sexual has obtained such a strong foothold in the theatre. A number of older players with whom I have discussed this point all agree that thirty years ago a company was unlikely to have more than one homosexual.

It was during the first World War, when many amateur shows were organized among the troops, with men playing women's parts, that homosexuals got their chance. This was the first war fought by a conscript army and it was inevitable that among such a vast number of conscripts there should be many homosexuals. They came into contact with professional actors who had also been conscripted, and found themselves in touch with professional organizers of army entertainments. It was inevitable that they should take advantage of these associations to try and get onto the professional stage after demobilization. Not only were the more artistic and talented given a chance on the dramatic stage, but others who were merely clever exhibitionists or female impersonators were able to get engagements in the world of lighter entertainment.

Today there are so many homosexuals in the British theatre that one young actor has this to say on the subject:

"When I go into a company I find it safest to assume that every male there is a homosexual until I have proof that he is not. I count myself lucky if I find there is one normal man among them."

Contrast this with the recollections of an actress of thirty years' experience:

"When I first went into the theatre at the end of the first World War I did not even know what homosexuality was. An older actress who shared my dressing room told me there was a homosexual in the company. We used to whisper and giggle about him. The company was not very friendly toward him and the whole thing was very hush-hush. Now homosexuals are quite candid about themselves. They have affairs with each other in the company and are accepted by everyone."

Among a mixed group of players there was great hilarity when, as a result of a particularly publicized scandal, there was a rumor that homosexuals were to be banned from the theatre. A young actor proclaimed that he would now be cast for boys' parts. A middle-aged man declared he would buy a toupee forthwith as he would be offered juvenile leads. Another man said, "It isn't a question of who would have to go if homos were banned but who would be left. There would certainly be jobs for everybody."

Another actor made this statement: "Not only is homosexuality generally prevalent but I know companies which are run, managed and directed by homosexuals in which no normal male can hope to obtain an engagement."

Any young actor at the beginning of his career is always fair game for the influential homosexual. If he does not respond, bitter hostility may result, as the following examples show.

A talented young actor went into a certain theatre with a special company. The resident manager told him that when that particular play had finished he would offer the youngster a part for the next production. Later the manager made homosexual advances. When there was no response he ceased to be friendly with the young man, and when the special week was finished curtly informed him that he would get no further work in that theatre. The young man's work was not at fault because he is seldom without an engagement.

Another young actor who had been too immersed in his work to be interested in women suddenly made a hit in a part and became a leading player. Being, as he thought, well established he cultivated a friendship with a girl and became engaged to be married. When the run ended, the young actor found that his former promoters were no longer interested in him. Because he had disappointed the homosexual who gave him his first big chance, the coterie were loud in their disapproval about how he had deceived and misled them.

Present laws and public opinion force homosexuals into a kind of secret society and this helps them inside the theatre. The people who help them may be victims of blackmail, moral or actual. Or they may simply be infatuated. Alternatively a successful actor who is a homosexual may offer advancement in the profession in return for the favors he desires.

Apart from these considerations, few managements will refuse work to a homosexual who is a good actor. If he is not, a homosexual employer will probably give him work in any case. Another aspect of the problem was put forward by a producer:

"The danger of the homosexual in the theatre is this. If a normal manager has some vacancies he is only interested in getting good actors. If a homo gets into a managerial position he will only employ his own kind. So when one homo gets in, others follow. I am not concerned with morals but I would put homos out of the theatre because they are a powerful and unscrupulous secret society."

A manager has this to say:

"Even if you tried, how could you keep out homosexuals? If you employed only married actors it is no guarantee that they are not homosexuals. People forget that Oscar Wilde was married and a father and this is not unusual."

An out-of-work actor had the following comment to make:

"I'm not a homosexual. I think the whole thing is damn

silly. I like women. But if a homo who can give me a good engagement propositions me again I may agree. So far as I can see it is the only way to get ahead in the theatre."

What has the homosexual actor himself to say? This is what one said to me:

"We get ahead on our own merits. We are more artistic, sensitive and perceptive than the ordinary male and that makes us better actors. Actresses often prefer us in a company. They know they have nothing to fear from us. It is the so-called normal actors who are jealous of us and want to get rid of us because we are better actors than they are. If that were not so we would not get engagements."

On the question of the way in which they help each other, another homosexual actor was perfectly frank:

"Of course we help each other. We have to because ordinary men are against us. In any case why should we not do so? What about that other powerful clique in the theatre, the university men? Every year they get into the theatre for no other reason than that they have the right social contacts. You know perfectly well many of them go straight into parts, even in London, when they leave university. They don't even have to go to a drama school."

This argument can scarcely be refuted. A young actor I knew went along, with several hundred others, to an audition. To his surprise he got the part. Later he discovered the producer had recognized his tie. There was a decade between them but they had both been to the same college at Oxford. What my homosexual friend did not mention, however, was that these two powerful influences may be linked. Homosexuality and a university education are not mutually exclusive.

There are other minority groups in the theatre and the homosexuals are not completely in control but they are undoubtedly very powerful. It is even doubtful if the word "minority" conveys an accurate picture of their numbers.

How true is their assertion that they are more sensitive and better actors than the normal male? In my experience they are neither better nor worse. The fact that they are homosexual has only one definite repercussion on their art. They cannot portray strongly male parts. In roles where such an interpretation is called for they may so reduce the emotional tone of the whole play that much of its impact is lost. This is particularly evident in certain Shakespearean roles. In comedy, homosexuals are often extremely successful.

There is something else to be considered. Not only are there homosexual actors but playwrights as well. The slant that the homosexual playwright has on humanity often inspires him to create characters which may be best portrayed by homosexual actors. During the past few years there have been many plays in which the homosexual has been portrayed as a comedy character which have been staged in purely commercial theatre. There have even been a few dramas in which the homosexual has been sincerely presented—or in which the plot turned on homosexual problems. Owing to the Lord Chamberlain's ban on this subject, such plays have been presented in club theatres and attracted large audiences because of the fascination of a forbidden topic. Now that the ban is lifted and a playwright who feels he has something to say about homosexuality can hope for acceptance of his play for ordinary theatres, there are likely to be more plays on this theme. It may be that there will be a spate of them, but once the novelty has worn off it is likely that the playwright will not seek to write a play with homosexual love as its theme any more than he is likely to write one with heterosexual love as his theme. People who fall in love and have emotional conflicts figure in most plays but the plot is usually concerned with other matters as well. In the future a homosexual character is likely to figure in plays on many themes simply because the homosexual exists and cannot be ignored.

There is no reason why a public which accepts stage characters with antisocial tendencies of all kinds should not gradually become more tolerant toward the homosexual character on the stage.

The lifting of the ban is likely to cause a curious situation in regard to casting. Homosexual actors are more suited to playing parts in which this human deviation is treated seriously and sympathetically. It remains to be seen if they will be cast for such parts. Normally sexed actors may fight shy of them.

In my questionnaire no direct inquiries were made regarding homosexuality, because this would not have elicited any worth-while information. The homosexual is so wary of any psychological probing that he shuns it. Some actors whom I knew were reluctant to fill in the questionnaire at all. There was, however, in many of the replies from the profession at large, indirect evidence of homosexuality. This was to be detected in expressions of opinion prevalent among homosexual actors such as criticism of the sexual element in plays, particularly in light comedy, and a desire for plays with a greater mystical content.

The reason for the latter wish was perhaps explained by a homosexual friend with whom I discussed the matter:

"We are already accepted in the theatre on our own merits and the time is coming when we shall be accepted by society. We are not in need of psychological treatment to make us what is stupidly called normal. We are a third sex and should be recognized as such. The feelings we have are much deeper and more spiritual than the so-called love between men and women. That is not love at all but simply animal emotion. I am absolutely convinced that the ordinary male does not know the first thing about real love and has never experienced it. On the stage we can convey much more tender and delicate emotions."

This particular actor, whom we shall call Vivian, talked to me with considerable frankness. He had been completely homosexual from the earliest age and had no close friends among women. When he was at dramatic school he had been sent to a psychiatrist. After a few sessions the psychiatrist evidently decided that the case was not suitable for treatment and advised Vivian to accept himself as he was and try to compromise with a world which was not of his way of thinking. His subsequent history does not suggest any great ability to compromise. Although he had very considerable talent he had to leave the drama school. He suffered from extreme anxiety and a lack of confidence in himself, in his work and in other people. He was extremely egotistical, suspicious and, at times, violent. His character was unsuited to group living. He was always seeking the perfect love object but no one could ever live up to his demands for an all-absorbing devotion.

If homosexual associations are doomed by their very nature to be undermined by jealousy, promiscuity and violence, the emotionally charged atmosphere of the theatre can only foster them. Here is one manager's view:

"Homosexuals always make trouble back stage. They are petty minded, jealous and inveterate mischief-makers. They are nearly always promiscuous. The way they carry on makes a bad atmosphere in the company. I would keep them out of the theatre if I had the power to do it."

If it is true that the homosexual is permanently at an immature emotional level, and that the actor is compelled by a particularly strong primitive emotion to choose the theatre as a way of life, so the homosexual actor—because he is emotionally immature—is often less well able to deal with his own personal problems than the normally sexed actor. Yet because theatre people are extremely tolerant of the failings of their own associates the homosexual in the acting profession meets with less open disapproval than he might meet with in other walks of life. But undoubtedly the homosexual actor may cause disharmony that can create a bad atmosphere in a theatre company.

It is often said that the homosexual actor should sacrifice his inclinations for the sake of his career and so avoid bringing the theatre into fresh disrepute. The homosexual's answer is to point to offenses, such as seduction and adultery, committed by heterosexual members of the profession.

The homosexual does not regard himself as a danger to society but as its victim. To all the charges made of promiscuity, violence, quarrels and mischief-making he has only one reply—that if he were accepted by society, all these unpleasant by-products of his life pattern would cease to exist. All he asks is to be liked and accepted as part of the society in which he lives. He never has regarded his behavior as antisocial.

Suggestions have been made that Equity, the actors' trade union, should refuse membership to homosexuals. That would be to throw the baby out with the bath water. No good actor should be debarred from acting because of his private life, unless he is a real social menace. Apart from this, the burden of proof would be too great for an organization such as Equity to undertake it. Even the police force, with all its resources, has to move most carefully in regard to homosexual offenders. It is difficult to obtain legal proof and still more difficult to bring about a conviction in court.

Individual theatrical managements could impose sanctions if they wished to do so. They do not have to give reasons for refusing a job to an actor. If, for instance, repertory managements reduced the number of homosexuals they employ, the total number in the theatre would soon be much less than it is today. Repertory is the main gateway to employment in the British theatre. Yet managements have little incentive for any action against the homosexual as far as public feeling is concerned. Sooner or later a manager will get rid of a troublemaker, irrespective of his sexual tendencies, and he will not engage anyone of unsuitable appearance or with strange mannerisms. Such a person could never play a wide variety of roles. So an actor who is obviously homosexual is not likely to be engaged except for specially suitable roles.

Audiences are seldom aware that an actor is homosexual through watching his stage performances. Only the more sophisticated may surmise that homosexuality is the reason why some virile male role is underplayed. Many of the romantic idols of the wider public have been or are homosexuals. There is no doubt that many women theatregoers are attracted by the acting of certain homosexuals, just as in the past women were attracted by the troubadours and their cult of nonphysical love. Most historians now agree that the troubadours did not have any physical relationship with the objects of their affections. Whether the troubadours were or were not active homosexuals is a point about which there is a great deal of dispute.

Whatever the truth of the troubadour's personal tendencies, the cult of romantic love has become part of our culture. The homosexual actor can portray certain types of highly sensitive characters, he may have a greater perception and sense of romantic artistry than the heterosexual actor possesses. These qualities in themselves do not make the homosexual a greater actor, but they do make him particularly appealing to women whose sex lives are frustrated or barren of romance. Until a series of public scandals makes women theatregoers aware of the less pleasant aspects of actors who are in fact homosexuals, these actors will continue to hold female patrons in thrall.

Another curious psychological fact is that while the homosexual often shines as a romantic lover, partly because of his own emotional make-up and partly because his approach to women is uncomplicated in many ways, the male actor is often shy of such roles. For at least thirty years the theme of romantic love has fallen into disfavor. No serious playwright of today would dare to write a play around a great love story. The word "love" has been largely replaced by the word "sex." "Love" is now regarded as the stuff of musical comedy. The popular "realism" of the past thirty years has replaced romance in serious drama. Nevertheless there are a great many theatregoers—mainly women—who still hunger for romance, even if it is only the vicarious romance of a stage performance.

The homosexual actor has a natural inclination toward the romantic, as opposed to the so-called realism of today. Therefore any suggestion that large commercial managements should ban the homosexual actor who shines in romantic roles whenever they do happen to be available, is impractical.

The greatest antagonism toward the homosexual actor is undoubtedly felt by actors who resent the influence exerted by the so-called third sex. This influence not only militates against the employment of heterosexual actors but may impede their progress once they are employed. While to those outside the theatre the employment of homosexual actors may be a moral problem, to those inside the theatre it is becoming an economic problem of ever-increasing intensity.

There is a possibility that the situation might improve if homosexuality ceased to be an indictable offense and homosexuals ceased to feel that they were a persecuted minority. To begin with, blackmail, either moral or actual, would stop if homosexual partners were no longer partners in crime. When irregular heterosexual relationships were privately tolerated but publicly condemned, blackmail was much more prevalent than it is today. In the theatre of the past, wealthy men often bought their way in as backers in order to obtain a part for a mistress in an effort to compensate her for her ignominious position. In these days of greater toleration such compensation is seldom necessary. Backers are more generally businessmen with an eye for a profitable investment.

If homosexuality were no longer regarded as a crime, homosexuals would cease to be a secret society and, to a very great extent, stop helping each other in the theatre as they do at present.

In the United States the influence of homosexuals in the theatre is somewhat limited for the simple reason that there is no widespread repertory theatre movement at present. In England, practically all fledgling actors start their careers in repertory theatres in order to gain experience and among these young people there are, of course, numbers of homosexuals. If some of these youngsters pass quickly from repertory to other theatres through favor rather than outstanding talent, they may be at least adequate actors. It is not unknown for a youngster to go from drama school straight into a part in a play in a London theatre either through influence, luck or talent, but it is not at all usual.

What is true of homosexuals as a group, both in England and the United States, is that they tend to be far less discreet than they were in the past. Prior to the war both American and British homosexual actors whom I knew did not discuss homosexuality with other people and were reticent in their behavior. One aspect of this lack of discretion is of course that while a minority movement within any community can exert power and influence to give personal help to its members, a majority movement cannot. A cake can be made to go just so far however thinly it may be sliced. The more obvious the behavior of homosexuals in any branch of the profession, the more attractive the profession will appear to other homosexuals. This could lead to bitter competition within the group, with resultant dissensions and betrayals that would ultimately weaken its power.

CHAPTER six

THE ACTOR AS A CITIZEN

The actor is sometimes accused of being neurotic because he has "escaped" into another world, the world of the theatre. That word "escape" is misused. Is it an "escape" to earn a living doing something you like doing, instead of something you dislike? If this is so, why are doctors, scientists and inventors not accused of escaping? They also have come to their careers not only because of a conscious desire to serve humanity, but as a result of the same kind of deep, unconscious emotional drive which influenced the actor in his choice of career.

One of the reasons why the actor is accused of being an escapist is to be found in Western man's terrible spiritual dilemma. Everything that has beauty and grace, even when the hardest work is needed to sustain it, is regarded as of less value than "practical things."

In addition to this false sense of values there is another misconception. We find it difficult to accept that some people possess strong emotional drives which set them apart from absorption in the usual preoccupations of economic man. Those who insist on their rights as individuals, instead of becoming part of a herd, are often labeled neurotics. Yet the would-be actor who is frustrated—and neurotic as a result—may become a happy and useful member of society if he achieves his ambition to act. The working actor gives much to society, but if forced into other employment he too may become neurotic and give little.

What is a well-balanced personality? Is it someone who is precariously adjusted to a way of life he would not choose, or a person who is happy in a way of life he has chosen—but which does not conform to an approved social pattern?

Who contributed most to society in the family of the Shakespeares? Was it his father, who made good gloves for those who could afford them and who was a worthy family man, or William, who refused to go into his father's business and left his wife and child in order to go to London and work in the theatre? Public opinion of the time condemned William when he went away and only reversed this judgment (or qualified it) when he became a success. In a similar situation today, commonly accepted psychological grading would place the elder Shakespeare as a well-adjusted personality and the young son William as maladjusted and probably neurotic.

In judging who is well adjusted and who is not we sometimes look through the wrong end of the telescope. As a group, actors come extremely low in the list of offenders against the law, whether in regard to crimes involving property or in acts of violence. This seems to prove that actors have adapted themselves to their environment.

Those who really are actors and earn their living by

acting usually have no criminal tendencies, for they are neither violent nor materialistic. Indeed the therapeutic value of acting is recognized by educators and psychologists. Acting plays a large part in adult education and "play therapy" has become an established form of treatment both for maladjusted children and certain types of neurotic adults.

The therapeutic value of acting is obvious if it is remembered that aggression is energy which has been misdirected into psychopathic channels. Energy can be directed toward positive creative ends or negative and destructive ones. Actors are the happy possessors of an excellent outlet for this vital force. Even when an actor behaves unconventionally he seldom has unconventional ideas or beliefs, only emotions that get out of hand. No one whose first desire is for the applause and love of a large mass of people is likely to have ideas and principles that are absolutely in conflict with those of the society within which he lives.

Nor are actors unmindful of the debt they owe to society and their families. One question in my questionnaire was, "What would you do if you inherited a large fortune?" Every actor or actress whose parents were living wanted to buy a house for them if they did not already own one, or to give them a large part of the money to ensure a comfortable old age. If neither of these were needed, they wanted to give their parents a holiday or expensive presents. As children most of us had daydreams of doing these things but in later life such aspirations usually fade away. Few of us keep alive the child within us as the actor does.

The remainder of the fortune was to be spent in various ways. The men usually wanted to build or buy their own theatre and finance their own theatre company. Some who were married wanted to buy a home of their own. Actresses wished to spend some of the money in ways that were the same as those of other women (I was able to compare their replies with replies to the same question made by women not connected with the stage). A number of actresses were prepared to leave the stage if a fortune came their way. In no case did anyone express the desire to spend the money on riotous living. The desire to do this was expressed by many nontheatrical people of both sexes when they gave their answers to this question.

Although the actor can and does sublimate his antisocial emotions in his art, the theatre has always been the whipping boy of the society of its day, the scapegoat of prevailing emotions. Since the actor is inseparable from the theatre, he is also something of a scapegoat. Sometimes he is confused with the characters he plays. An actor I knew, who was playing Danny in *Night Must Fall,* noticed on taking a taxi that the driver seemed wary and rather apprehensive. At the journey's end the actor chatted cheerfully for a few minutes and the driver exclaimed, "Coo, you aren't like Danny at all reely."

Yet plays in which the leading character is very antisocial have always been popular. Despite this, few actors are really happy in a career of villainous roles. I know one actor who made an enormous success in such parts but gradually came to dislike them more and more. He craved for parts in which he would portray virtuous characters and turned down part after part because the lead offered was "not a nice person." Since his physical appearance was not suited to the type of character he wished to play, he gradually fell into oblivion. The younger generation of playgoers would scarcely recognize his name.

I know another actor who became famous as a polished villain in films and eventually left Hollywood because he could not obtain other types of part. Charles Laughton, at one time the most famous of stage and screen villains, eventually broke away from such roles in order to play very different types of part. On the other hand, I cannot recall any actor who has deliberately forsaken either stage or screen because he tired of playing virtuous characters.

Intense as is the actor's desire to be "a good child of society," and removed as he is from many of the temptations that assail other types of citizen, he should learn not to be oversensitive about the characters he portrays. The public may confuse the actor with his roles but the actor should not fall into this trap. He will not become a better citizen through always portraying virtue nor a worse one if he often portrays vicious, antisocial characters.

One reason why the actor may be inclined to be oversensitive in regard to the types of part he plays is that he has little opportunity to mix with the world at large. If he is working in repertory he rehearses during the day and performs in the evening. So he sees little of anyone outside the theatre. If he is playing in a long run his leisure hours are during the day when the mass of people work. Therefore his great link with society as a whole is through his acting and he knows the public will associate him with the roles he plays.

In the case of the English repertory actor, this can have one curious repercussion. His audiences know and recognize him, and during his hurried dashes from theatre to lodgings and back will stop him in the street to talk with him. If he happens to be playing the part of a poet they will almost certainly talk to him about poetry. If he is playing a clergyman, the local clergy of all denominations will chat on church matters and fully expect the actor to be conversant with the subject. On one occasion when I produced a play about a chef, members of the audience who were in the catering trade always stopped the actor playing the part in order to pour out reminiscences about chefs they had known and culinary matters. Although the repertory actor has a great fondness for his public, this kind of thing can become so irksome that members of a repertory actor has a great fondness for his public, this quiet back streets rather than walk along main thoroughfares at lunch hour.

An unpleasant characteristic attributed to the actor as a private citizen is that he is an exhibitionist. Nothing, however, could be further from the truth in most instances. A great number of actors, including stars, walk about city streets every day almost unnoticed except by other members of the profession. It is among drama students, intoxicated by their new status, that exhibitionism prevails. Exhibitionism at premières or social occasions is another matter. It is part of the involved business of getting ahead in an overcrowded profession.

If exhibitionism is confused with the actor's desire to be the center of attention on a lighted stage, then the actor is an exhibitionist; but what he does is the highest form of sublimation. It must also be remembered that unless an actor is a very influential star he has to accept the parts he is offered. Sometimes therefore he has to play the part of a character who is an exhibitionist. Also, an actor may often have to appear in plays which, as a private citizen, he would condemn. There is an audience for plays that a considerable section of the public denounces on moral or aesthetic grounds.

There is a section of the public which will disapprove of certain plays because of the sexual content. They do not realize that they may be treading on dangerous ground. The actor should realize this. Where the taboo on sex becomes excessive we can have a very undesirable tendency in dramatic art and one which does exist today. That is the suppression of the romantic aspects of sexual attachments and the isolation of the purely functional aspects of sex. Some modern American playwrights are tending to do this and English ones are now inclined to follow this trend. Man has inherent romantic feelings, and if social attitudes or social systems strive to detach these from sexuality a new danger can arise. Man's sense of romance may attach itself to another atavistic instinct, the instinct to fight, to be a warrior.

It has been noted by anthropologists that warrior tribes do not produce great art nor do nations with warlike traditions. In modern times we had an example of this in Nazi Germany, where art not only ceased to flourish but was actively suppressed. In other words, vital forces were deliberately directed toward one form of outlet— aggression and conquest. Creative art is a sublimation of primitive instincts, sex and aggression. These instincts are common to all, even the best of good citizens. If sexual expression is repressed or debased, art withers away. It may be true that in both the United States and Great Britain there are theatrical entertainments based on the crudest kind of sexual appeal, but the general taste of theatregoers as a whole is not in this direction, nor is it likely to be. Quite apart from other factors involved, each year sees greater numbers of women in theatre audiences because they can now afford to buy their own seats. The less intellectual ones may prefer romantic comedies to serious dramas but they are not attracted by crude sexual display.

So, however much the actor may desire to be a good citizen, he should not condemn entertainment that deals with sex in a silly or vulgar way too vehemently. He should instead seek to hasten the movement toward a better type of play which treats human love and sexuality along more imaginative lines. The bedroom farces that caricature human emotions are still with us, although in declining numbers. At the opposite end of the pole many so-called realistic plays oversimplify these same emotions.

CHAPTER seven

THE ACTOR AND THE PUBLIC

The actor's feelings toward his public are just as ambivalent as are the feelings of the public toward the actor, although the emphasis is different. To the public the successful actor is a fabulous freak to be admired, acclaimed and envied. He is expected to open magic casements but never to let in disturbing drafts. He must be godlike but at the same time as easily comprehensible as the next-door neighbor.

Interest in actors has never been so great as it is today—a phenomenon for which the vast machinery of publicity is responsible. Every actor knows he needs his fans but the fans' adulation is composed of both love and hate.

I once had the opportunity of studying hundreds of fan letters sent to a young woman star. Among them was a long and particularly saccharine love letter written by a man in his twenties (for some reason fans of both sexes invariably mention their ages). This letter had been mislaid and a second letter arrived a few months later. It was full of invective and the writer threatened to attend a performance and make trouble because the first letter had not been answered.

It is not surprising that the star's emotions toward his fans are like those of a lion tamer toward his lions. In either case a single slip may cause disaster. Most fans are not lovers of drama. They will go to see a favorite star and, even when inside the theatre, not always know the name of the play. A film player who appears in the theatre often has to undergo the irritating experience of hearing part of the audience of film fans leave as the play draws toward its close, as is customary with audiences in the cheaper movie houses.

At the same time, although stars are well aware of the ambivalence of fan emotions, they do not always realize that fan influence is corrupting. Few stars escape the unhealthy influence of fan idolatry altogether. Applause and acclaim are the breath of life to the actor but the breath can carry poison. The star represents the fans' daydreams of what they themselves would like to be. That is why, while fulfilling the fan's daydreams, the star is expected to remain a simple person at heart. So any intelligent interests in the arts or any symptoms of cultivated taste are likely to alienate the fan. Identification goes further. While liking to think that the star's life is a glamorous whirl of gaiety among the world's celebrities, the fan will write a note beginning, "I expect you remember me. I came to see you when you opened in Hickville two years ago." Or, "You may remember I asked you for your autograph when you played in Coaltown last year."

No wonder that, to the actor, his audience is a fairy godmother, a humble worshiper, a terrifying ogre, a moron, a Philistine, a stern father and a loving mother. It is to be both loved and feared.

The child of stage parents who becomes a star is, from the beginning, acutely aware of the apparent contradictions in the attitude of the audiences. Because he knows the contradictions so well he may develop contempt for audiences, or an eternal vigilance. I have known stars who have such a fear of offending fans that they are never free from anxieties.

To the youngster unacquainted with the ambivalence of fan reactions, fan worship can seem one of the most rewarding aspects of theatrical life. Such a youngster may desire to be a star with a vast fan following rather than to be a really good actor. This was so in the case of a young man I shall call Norman.

Norman came from a lower middle-class background and was indulged from an early age because of his striking good looks and intelligence. He had an unusually good record at school and a successful career of some sort seemed assured. Norman was anxious to get on in the world. At eighteen he had such a fine physique that the doctors who passed him for national service remarked on it.

In uniform Norman looked more striking than ever and his comrades assured him that he would have no trouble in becoming a film star. Norman, who had never had any interest in any of the arts, was delighted. A film star's existence would suit him very well.

However, Norman was no fool. When he came out of the service he decided to start by having some dramatic training and then to get some stage experience before taking off for the film studios. Nevertheless several years in full-time drama school seemed a waste of time to someone like him with all his natural assets. To some extent this was true. The young man began part-time training, managed to attract the attention of a producer and within a few weeks obtained a semiprofessional engagement. Through the efforts of his coach Norman did surprisingly well. He lapped up lessons in voice production and stage movement, had the ability to take direction and had sufficient intelligence to do exactly what he was told. From a few weeks of semiprofessional work he went into a repertory theatre.

A few months afterwards he met a businessman whose hobby was theatre, and who assured Norman that he would make him a star. All he asked in return was that Norman should break his existing contract with his coach. Since it was not the kind of contract Equity would uphold, it was unlikely that the coach would take the matter to law. Norman blithely broke the contract.

Six months later the self-appointed impresario found that his theatre was losing money so he cut his losses and closed down. Norman was out of work. To him the cultural and historical aspects of the theatre were so unknown that they scarcely existed. Except for some enforced study at school he knew nothing of Shakespeare. He had no background of knowledge to sustain him.

Some years have passed. Engagements have been few and film producers have remained uninterested. Norman does not understand why other young actors who do not have his physique or looks, or even the smart clothes he buys, are given engagements while he is not. In many ways his good looks were his worst enemy. But for them no one would have suggested that he should contemplate a theatrical career, since he does not have the psychology of the true actor. Even his facile ability to learn was unfortunate, because it masked the fact that he had no love of learning for its own sake but only for the satisfaction of his vanity.

He could not succeed—he was not drawn toward acting out of any deep emotional need to act but because he wanted to be a popular idol.

The theatre will not serve everybody's ends. The aspiring actor who brings to it everything it needs can count himself fortunate if he is allowed to serve it.

The newly fledged actor is usually idealistic and if he thinks about fans at all is likely to take it for granted that he will win them through talent and integrity. He is often shocked by the intense rivalry between individual performers in a company. To him the audience is "they" and the players "us" and it is unthinkable that there should not be complete teamwork among the small group on the stage in the face of that large crowd in the auditorium. Unfortunately, absolute teamwork never has prevailed and never can prevail in the highly commercialized theatre, where every man is out for himself and no holds are barred. In capital cities an assortment of aggressive and obvious solo performances may be rare, but there is a rivalry of a more subtle kind although the audience is unaware of it. On tours and in small companies the rivalry may often be crude and obvious.

The actor who is an artist and a well-adjusted personality comes to terms with his fellow players and with his audience. He knows he has his part to play and that his fellow actors have theirs. He also knows that the audience has a positive contribution to make. In this respect, however, audiences vary not only in different towns, but from one night to the next. Most actors will, as a team, do what they can to counteract "the rot" if they feel a lack of audience response. If certain players overdo this extra effort, however, the play will suffer. Few plays fail because of apathy on the part of anyone concerned with their production. Failures more often result from overanxiety, and the consequent frenzied personal efforts to put things right. This sometimes happens when a play has been a success in a big city and fails to go over elsewhere.

With experience every actor learns how unpredictable his public can be. A first-night audience in a capital city presents special problems. It is likely to be composed of people who make a point of going to first nights, for various reasons. Some say they like to see the play on a first night because they can then form their own opinion of it uninfluenced by the opinion of the professional critics. Others go because it is a social occasion. This group is likely to give the play a good reception and perhaps not be very critical. Then there are the fans who have come to see a favorite actor or actress and they may either like or dislike the play itself. There are the people who get enjoyment out of being unnecessarily critical, the sort of people who put on an act of their own so that their reactions and remarks cannot go unnoticed by those around them.

Then there are the professional critics, who are in a class by themselves. It may truly be said that anything that can be said about critics anywhere is likely to be true about a critic somewhere. They may praise or blame, they may be ignorant or well informed. Being human they are likely to have prejudices for or against certain types of plays or players. No wonder first nights are such an ordeal for the actors.

Yet neither audience reaction nor the critics' reports of a first night necessarily decide the fate of a play. It may have been well received, but this is no guarantee that it will have a successful run. If its reception has not been very good this does not necessarily mean failure. For instance, there are many comedies and some dramas which were badly received by the professional critics in London yet have quite literally run for years; several are doing so at present. The explanation of such successes is not always to be found in star names or superlative performances. Even when a play has settled down to a steady run, audience reaction will not be the same night after night. These variations in audience reaction affect the actor in the same way that stubbing his toe on an unexpected stone affects a pedestrian. It is disconcerting when a joke which has hitherto got a big laugh fails to do so and also disconcerting when this is followed by laughter over a joke which has not gone down too well previously. Most jarring of all, of course, are the occasions when there are a few giggles during a play which is not a comedy.

Naturally accomplished and experienced players are best able to control any slight contretemps. They can do this by sheer skill and weight of personality as a rule without portraying any reaction to whatever has momentarily upset the smooth progress of the performance. Today it is far more necessary to do this than it was in the past when the theatre enjoyed—or perhaps we should say suffered—less publicity than it does today. An old actor recently told me about an incident when he played with an old-time star. Some sadistic trait caused this star to purposely delay his entrances so that the players on the stage were forced to ad-lib. One night an actor did this to great effect. "The old b—— is late again," he exclaimed and went on to talk of something else.

Companies on tour often have unexpected difficulties with which to contend because mishaps are more likely to occur and these cannot always be covered up very easily.

The English repertory actor in a town where often the same people come to the theatre week after week usually amasses extraordinary knowledge of the reactions of his audiences. This is partly because most people are creatures of habit. They will go to the theatre on one special night. The company gets to know from experience the sort of audience reaction they may expect on the night "the carriage trade" elects to patronize the theatre as contrasted to the reactions from their audience on early closing day. Reactions will be different again if there is one evening when late buses are specially laid on to bring in people living in surrounding rural districts.

In this type of repertory the company is often made up of enthusiastic young actors whose freshness and integrity compensate for lack of experience. Usually there is a very friendly relationship between the actors and the audience.

A much less happy situation prevails in popular holiday resorts. The mass of the audiences will not be in the town for more than one or two weeks and quite a number are not regular theatregoers in any case. They may practically never go to a theatre except when they are on holiday. So they are likely to react to the play and to the acting just as they would to a situation in real life and the people in it. Whether one is on the stage or in the auditorium, one cannot help hearing remarks such as, "I bet *he* really done the murder!" "I don't know how he married anyone like her," and "He's going to get a surprise in a minute." There is complete identification of the actor with the part.

The more experienced theatregoers in such audiences are not usually amused by these remarks and they are seldom enthusiastic over the performances, because these may not be up to the standards to which such playgoers are accustomed. The players in such companies are usually better paid than in ordinary repertory theatres but the leads are often middle-aged and frustrated and have a blasé attitude. They have lost the power to kindle the imagination of any audience. They would not enjoy performing in a play which made any demand on their own understanding. To be able to stimulate an audience to greater perception is the true test of an actor's quality. The audience cannot be expected to assimilate new and original ideas if the actor does not help them to do so.

In both France and the United States "out-of-town" audiences are often better served. The summer theatres of the United States are likely to have players of all ages and stages of success. In addition, the standard of the plays presented is, on the whole, very much higher than those offered at English holiday resorts. This is partly due to the fact that American summer theatres are not catering only to tourists and vacationists as a rule but to the local population as well. In British holiday resorts, and particularly those by the sea, tourism is practically the only industry and supports most of the local population. The influx of holiday makers is so enormous that they make up at least ninety per cent of the theatre audiences. For some reason these audiences prefer—or at any rate get—an almost undiluted diet of crude farces and crime plays.

In France the leading theatrical companies leave Paris during the summer season and tour the provincial cities and large towns. In addition other, smaller, companies are organized to do the same thing every summer. In places that are purely holiday resorts, such as the Riviera or the northern coast, plays are seldom presented. The main sources of evening entertainments are the cafés and the ubiquitous casino.

CHAPTER eight

THE ACTRESS AND SOCIETY

Among actresses the response to my questionnaire was poor, about twenty per cent of the total of the forms returned. Except in a small number of cases the answers to the questions were perfunctory. This avoidance of, or apathy toward, self-analysis in the actress has been my experience of her in training and producing also. Among my pupils those who have worked hardest and most consistently have nearly all been men.

On the whole the young actress is less single-minded about her career, and romance or marriage is always likely to divert her from it. This attitude is not only a sexual characteristic of women but it has deep historical and social roots.

When the taboo against female performers on the stage was broken, the theatre was practically the only field in which women could compete with men on an equal basis. The only other types of employment open to women were badly paid and very humble. It was a reflection on the social standing of a family if daughters had to go out to work. Parents did their utmost to support daughters until such time as the most advantageous marriage possible could be arranged. So the first actresses were, unwittingly, the first group of women to break the chains that bound their sex to the kitchen and the cradle. They still form one of the largest sections of professional women in most of the countries in the Western world today.

The actresses who were pioneers had no clear-cut ideas about emancipation nor did they usually seek the stage as a result of some deep emotional compulsion to act, but for a variety of other reasons. The poor girl longed for a chance to wear pretty clothes and to enjoy a better standard of living. The girl with social ambitions saw in a theatrical career an opportunity to capture a wealthy, aristocratic husband, or lover. The girl with a drab, unhappy home saw glamour in life in the theatre. The romantic girl could see herself as a new and more potent Helen, or a Cleopatra who would never need to resort to the asp. The young women who went into the theatre belonged to several or even all of these categories.

When they left home to go into the theatre these women suffered social ostracism, and usually continued to do so unless they married into the aristocracy. They lived in a world of strictly masculine values and were considered fair game for exploitation. This was a period in which no respectable woman cared to appear in the streets alone during the day and would seldom dare to do so after dark.

The unscrupulous and cunning women could fight with the only weapon they possessed, sexual charm. One of the most graphic accounts of the male attitude toward the actress—and the female stratagems that resulted—is to be found in Boswell's *London Journal*. The young Scotsman came to London to try to get a commission in the army and be able to boast that he had a London actress for a mistress. The account of his first serious affair reads more like records of war than love. Boswell is determined to seduce a young actress into becoming his mistress with as little expense to himself as possible; the actress, on the other hand, tries to extract as much as she can for small favors while protesting her chastity. In the end Boswell emerged without much damage to his pocket but with wounds to his vanity, the knowledge of having been fooled, and with a souvenir in the form of a dose of venereal disease.

The capture of a wealthy lover was the easiest way to success for the actress and to attain the position of mistress to the King was the greatest of all achievements. Even to become the mistress of a minor royalty was to reach dizzy eminence and continued to be regarded as such until quite modern times. While seeking to exploit, the actress was also exploited. Even if she was not amoral she was still beset by lovers who wanted to share her reflected glory or to profit by it.

In spite of the fact that a number of actresses did marry into aristocratic families, this war of the sexes was still to a great extent carried on outside the citadel of society and was a preoccupation of the demimonde. Society as a whole sat at secure vantage points to watch the battle and at the same time expressed deep disapproval of the protagonists.

For about two hundred years the conviction that woman's place was in the home, and that her functions were purely sexual, remained unshaken until it gradually began to split on the rocks of economic realities. Toward the end of the nineteenth century, daughters of impoverished middle-class families, as well as those of working-class families, began to look to the stage as a means of earning an honest living in an interesting sphere. Also the social rebel, who disliked the limitations of her role as a woman, saw in the theatre a weapon with which she could fight for emancipation and sexual as well as economic equality. The career of an actress no longer involved social ostracism, only some family disapproval or grief, and possibly a certain amount of social criticism.

The girl's entree into the theatre was still dependent on good looks or a pleasing personality or both. If she had talent all the better, but talent alone would not put her on the stage. The lighter stage bloomed and glowed with dozens of attractive young ladies who, if they did not achieve startling artistic success, often enjoyed amazing social success. Wealthy lovers were so easily acquired that they were now commonplace. It was in the marriage market that these girls sought fulfillment of their ambitions. To marry a peer was now a normal event; for real distinction, marriage to a duke was the thing.

This state of affairs continued until the nineteen twenties; a glittering myth had been created by "the Gaiety girls," "the girls from Daly's," "Mr. Cochran's Young Ladies" and Florenz Ziegfeld's beauties. Very large numbers of them married into the aristocracy. Then, as noble rank tended to become an expensive liability rather than an asset, stage beauties began to look with calculation upon the plutocrat rather than the aristocrat. When a romantic girl, an ambitious girl or a dissatisfied girl turns to a stage career she still hopes to improve her standard of living or her social status, irrespective of her talent. Even if she comes from a comfortable middle-class home and a secure social background, the environment of the theatre still seems to offer romantic fulfillment of a kind for which her male counterpart has no desire.

What the romantically inclined girl has to remember is

that the theatre has changed. The theatre is now a highly competitive business. Gone are the days when a wealthy man would back a show in order to star a young actress with whom he was in love, gone too the stage-door Johnnies and the champagne drunk from slippers. Good looks and charm are not enough to ensure either an advantageous marriage or theatrical success. In the world of light entertainment a high standard of ability is expected from the musical comedy actress.

Although it was because of her sex rather than her art that woman was originally allowed into the theatre, profitable exploitation of sex was not the motif for this revolution. The pressure for females to play female roles originally came from French playwrights who felt that this was a necessary step. It was the exiled playwrights and actors who fled to France during the Puritan interregnum and who saw actresses perform in the French theatre, who later introduced the actress to the English stage. It is difficult to imagine how the boy players of Shakespeare's day fulfilled the playwright's intentions. A boy playing Cleopatra would now seem incredible. Lady Macbeth may have been less of a problem; it is almost the only great female role ever written in which lust for power is the central theme and sex relationships are scarcely touched upon. It is not surprising that most of the great roles in Elizabethan dramas were for males.

Since drama first existed, male roles have called for the portrayal of almost every variation of human emotions. But because of society's attitude to women the dramatist has always looked upon his heroine as a sexual object or has written his plot around some aspect of her sex life. This trend was most marked toward the end of the nineteenth century and the beginning of the twentieth century in the plays of Sutro and Pinero and many other fashion-

able playwrights. Even George Bernard Shaw, the dramatist who regarded himself as a social rebel, wrote along
these lines. The difference was that Shaw, with his fear of
sex, went a step further than previous playwrights. He
created female characters with brains, ability and dynamic drive, set them up like Humpty Dumpty on walls of
reason, so that their ultimate fall was all the greater, and
further humiliated them by causing them to turn into
Titanias when they hit the ground. These heroines fell,
not for the noble heros beloved of past dramatists, nor for
the polished seducer or the cunning villain, but for asses.
Furthermore these unromantic males were generally recognized as asses by the other characters in the play as well
as by the female victims of the biological urge. Candida
loved two men, both of whom she knew to be her in-
feriors; Eliza was prepared to throw away her future
when the neurotic Higgins boggled at accepting his role
as a male; and the heroine of *The Doctor's Dilemma* en-
slaved herself to a poet, replicas of whom could be found
by the dozen in Chelsea or Greenwich Village.

As the modern playwright is practically always preoccupied with the presentation of male problems, the star role
is more likely to be for an actor than an actress. One of
the few successful modern plays in which the leading
role is for an actress is *The Deep Blue Sea,* although here
again the drama centers around the woman infatuated
with an unsuitable man. In the United States, playwrights
do tackle bigger themes. In *Anna Christie* Eugene O'Neill
came nearest to the insight Ibsen showed in *The Doll's
House.* Yet O'Neill's background and experience made
him give his play an inherently tragic ending, for no one
with any understanding could imagine that a future
with Matt will hold any hope of fulfillment for Anna.
Ibsen's Nora had that hope. Nevertheless O'Neill was

aware that women could not continue to remain in traditional niches as sexual objects. Tennessee Williams is also preoccupied with women, but the world in his plays is in decay, and all his characters, both male and female, can only destroy themselves and each other.

For historical and social reasons it is not surprising that there have been few actresses of comparable stature to the greatest actors. This is also true today. Many famous actresses have been women with a great deal of feminine charm, vivacity and vitality who have gradually learned a technique of acting which successfully exploits their own personalities. The highest achievements in the art of acting can usually be attributed to actresses who have reached or passed middle age. They are no longer preoccupied with their personal emotional lives, and society has learned to value them for their qualities as individual artists. Time has perfected their technique and developed their imaginations.

It seems a pity that more playwrights do not realize this fact. A playwright who writes a play in which a young girl has to carry a very important part is offering a hostage to fortune. If he writes a play in which a middle-aged or elderly woman plays the leading role he is on far safer ground. The extraordinarily long runs enjoyed by a number of mediocre plays in which Marie Tempest appeared in her later years are good examples of what the older actress can achieve.

The cinema has had an unfortunate effect on casting. Because of their youthful freshness, young girls with little acting ability are starred in leading roles. Many of these young women get little chance to develop, although of course a few do gradually become character actresses and retain stardom into middle age. This tendency in the film studios—to give leading parts to inexperienced young actresses—has also affected the theatre. In the past, great parts were given to great actresses who could still look youthful. Possibly modern publicity methods are partly responsible for the change, because the age of an actress is likely to be quoted over and over again so the public is much more aware of the age of any well-known actress than it was in the past.

It is significant, however, that the most experienced of British playwrights, Noël Coward, has never written his biggest and longest parts for the very young girl. His plays have leading roles for the more mature woman and less demanding parts for the very young woman. In the United States the type of plays written by the best playwrights usually exclude this problem. The plays are stronger than those by British authors of the older age group and demand a high standard of teamwork rather than the presence of one or two stars. Naturally stars are an asset from the box office angle but most star actresses are of mature age.

The difference in the time needed for the actress to achieve true artistry and secure a niche in the temple of fame, and that needed by the actor to reach the same status, is obvious when comparisons are made. In England, Sir Laurence Olivier and Sir John Gielgud reached their full artistic maturity in their early thirties. Most of those who are at their heels are between twenty-five and thirty. In the United States, Fredric March and Alfred Lunt were artistically mature by the age of thirty and the late John Barrymore slightly earlier.

In England our greatest dramatic actresses—Peggy Ashcroft and Dame Sybil Thorndyke—were about forty when they reached their full powers. The same was true of the internationally famous Lynn Fontanne who, although English by birth, must be considered an American actress.

Statistics show that women live longer than men and usually enjoy greater health in their later years. This has an affect on theatre players. Few actors give greater performances than previously in their later years, although they usually retain and enrich the quality of their art. But actresses over forty usually make great advances. They may have been hampered by their sex in early development of intellect. Their full powers, once attained, seem unimpaired until very late in life.

It is to be hoped that in the future the emotional overtones attached to the question of woman's place in the world will continue to change. As the stresses and conflicts engendered by social attitudes become less acute, the woman artist will realize that the characteristics that divide her from the male artist are socially imposed rather than innate. She may understand that the fact that she is an artist is of far deeper significance than the physical and psychological differences between men and women.

Once the young actress ceases to believe that her sex makes her the victim of a tragic dichotomy, artistic maturity may come to her earlier. If she refuses to accept traditional social values without question, tries to understand herself better and is persistent in her search for self-awareness, then her whole position will be improved.

CHAPTER nine

THE PSYCHOLOGY OF THE ACTRESS

In spite of society's attitude toward the woman artist, the girl's first steps toward a theatrical career are often easier than for the boy, providing her parents have no violent prejudice against the theatre. This is not because parents believe that it is easier for a girl to succeed in the theatre but because they are more indulgent toward her whims and fancies. They may be skeptical about her talent or her prospects but this is not so important as a good marriage later on. There is a feeling that a stage training may make a girl more attractive and increase her opportunities for making a suitable marriage, or even a far better marriage than might otherwise be likely. Actresses do learn to speak and move nicely and to develop charm of manner, all of which makes them attractive to the opposite sex.

The child who wants to become an actress is likely to start off by dressing up in her mother's old clothes and indulging in make-believe. This is not likely to meet with disapproval and may be regarded as charming and amusing. If, as sometimes happens, the mother has had a frustrated desire for a theatrical career she may encourage her daughter's ambition to become an actress. She will see in an actress daughter a vicarious fulfillment of her own dreams. Occasionally the mother will go further. She will decide that her daughter must become an actress. I have seen girls, some of them very unpromising material, literally forced into training and performing at a very early age. One sulky youngster, who at that time loathed attending a drama class and whom one longed to send home, is now quite a well-known actress.

Many actresses have family connections with the theatre and owe their first start to such connections. In the past a number of actresses were spared the conflicts and struggles that confront the aspiring actress of today because they came of theatrical families. Far from having to meet family opposition when they sought stage careers, the parents took it for granted that their daughters would go into the theatre and the youngsters began as performers as soon as possible, often making their debut as babes carried onto the stage in scenes where a baby was required. Such children would have aroused family disapproval if they had not taken to stage careers and when the time came for marriage, the parents would probably have been deeply grieved if the girls chose husbands outside the theatre.

These were the days of the stock companies with casts consisting of parents and their children and very often other relatives as well. Outsiders in such companies were generally in a minority and in many cases did not remain outsiders as they were likely to marry a son or daughter of the actor-manager. Sara Siddons, Duse, Ellen Terry and Ethel Barrymore came from families such as this. At that time school attendance was not compulsory, so the children of these theatrical folk grew up in a self-contained little world. The girls were able to conform to the society around them, to be like everyone else, because the backstage of the theatre was the only society they knew. Marriage did not disrupt their careers if they married a member of the company nor did motherhood. They would act up to a few weeks before the birth of a child and soon afterward return to the stage. A cradle in a dressing room —or rather a baby in a theatrical skep—was no novelty.

Modern conditions have destroyed these theatrical dynasties. Theatrical parents often lead lives widely separated from those of their children, so that the children may have little real contact with the theatre. For instance, the children of a doctor are far more apt to follow in his footsteps than the children of theatrical parents are likely to go on the stage.

The star system has also affected the attitude of both the children and the parents. If a mother is a star, her daughter may feel that she could not compete with such formidable talent and will seek to express herself in some other way. If it is the father who is the star, then the situation is more favorable for the girl. Rivalry will not exist between father and daughter as it does between mother and daughter. A number of promising present-day young actresses are the daughters of male stars. Sons of male stars seldom venture into the theatrical profession and when they do they never seem to make a very great success.

It might be imagined that a mother who is a great actress would enjoy helping her son to a stage career but this does not seem to be so. In discussing the psychology of the successful actress, a psychiatrist told me that he had found one quality in common among all the actresses who had come to him for advice and that was an unconscious desire for power. He believed this had come about through their struggles with their own innate femininity. In order to succeed they had had to suppress female qualities that might have hindered them and to overcompensate for any possible weakness by being more ruthless than their male counterparts. For this reason they regarded all newcomers, male or female, as their rivals. In cases where their adolescent sons had expressed a desire for a stage career the relationship between mother and son often suffered greatly.

In adolescence both sexes are divided against themselves and often opposed to accepting the roles in which their social position and family environment have cast them. Unconsciously the would-be actress is in rebellion against her total situation. She may rebel against the powerful position the father holds in the family. She may resent the influence the mother has over the family, and in relation to the father. She may even resent the power of the male in the world as a whole. If this is so she will fight the power of the male by making use of her own particular weapons. She uses her sex to attain her ends. At the same time she is less self-conscious in her revolt than is the boy and therefore more disarming. She may zealously protect her fantasies and put up formidable defenses against the intrusion of reason.

The legend of Narcissus is Greek in origin and belonged to a society so deeply committed to masculine ideals that it was boys and not girls who were socially accepted as love objects and subjects of romantic adoration. If the psychoanalysts of the Western world were to rewrite the legend it might be a girl rather than a boy who would be the central figure. A Narcissa looking in a pool will see an idealized reflection of herself, possessing great beauty of body and spirit. For the girl, heroism is inappropriate.

After the Crimean War its heroine, Florence Nightingale, was regarded not so much as a great figure but as a tiresome old woman with a bee in her bonnet. Narcissa has to take refuge from herself in herself. She hopes for power not so much from what she does as from what she is.

If she abandons her fantasies and accepts her function in a patriarchal society as wife, mother and housekeeper, she cannot hope for recognition in her own right as an individual. She can only exist in relation to her husband, her children and her home. Man's individuality is recognized in his objective achievements as a maker, an active force. It is therefore inevitable that women tend to confine themselves to preoccupation with their physical appearance, and to be influenced only by their most immediate experiences. Woman has to give *herself* immense importance because she is made to feel inferior as far as objective attainment is concerned.

The stage-struck boy desires to identify himself with the heroic character he hopes to portray. The stage-struck girl can only hope to mirror her own perfections and to win acclaim while doing so. Practically all great female roles in drama are the apotheosis of conventional feminine perfections—or conventional feminine allure.

In describing the work of an actor, critics employ a wide vocabulary, but praise of an actress nearly always carries a sexual content and is expressed in words with a sexual connotation. "Charming," breathtaking," "enchanting," "lovely," "disarming," are in common usage. Sometimes a critic may even say that Miss So-and-So looked so beautiful that his critical judgment was suspended. In the past, performances by Miss Lynn Fontanne were frequently commended along these lines. It is only now, when she has proved that she can be equally impressive in old age, that critics begin to suspect that her fascination may have something to do with her art.

Because society's attitude to the female forces her to seek confidence in her own mirrored reflection, this mirror can become her whole world. The Lady of Shallott saw Sir Lancelot over her own shoulder in her mirror. That is, she saw her own romantic idealization of herself in her private mirror and a man behind her. On Halloween a girl is supposed to be able to see the shadowy figure of her future husband behind her if she gazes in her mirror. It was a girl and not a boy who got into the world of the looking glass, in the Lewis Carroll story.

Being both priestess and idol, worshiped and worshiper, Narcissa need only *be,* she does not need to impress herself upon externals. In fantasy all can be fulfilled. Even physical beauty is not indispensable to the fantasy because it is believed that charm may be as potent as beauty. When Narcissa is a plain, excessively shy and awkward creature she may be upheld by an inner conviction that she possesses a notably lovely soul.

Again, she may secure confidence from fantasies regarding her sexual appeal. In some cases her whole attitude to life is based on an assumption of sexual irresistibility. Armed with this conviction, securely entrenched in her fantasy, Narcissa may make her existence a sort of personal sacred drama.

It is no wonder that the theatre should attract Narcissa nor that every would-be actress is a Narcissa to some degree. Without this characteristic a girl might never have the courage to seek a stage career at all.

One interesting aspect of the female drama student's feelings about herself can be found in the kind of part she enjoys playing. A male student will revel in a role that makes him hideous, and will enjoy playing old men, the older and uglier the better. The boy is aware that age gives the male privileges and at the same time lessens responsibilities. Biologically and sexually no more is expected of the oldster, he may indulge himself in quirks and fads, he is a free soul. The old woman, on the other hand, is reduced in importance insofar as she ceases to be looked upon as a desirable sexual object. So every aspiring actress or drama student wants to play Juliet or Cleopatra —not merely because they are good parts but because when she looks in the secret mirror of her own fantasies she knows she is both the tragic heroine of Verona and the queen of the Nile.

The actor is unconsciously attempting to identify himself with characters of power and prestige, to play roles for which he might not be qualified in real life. The actress is unconsciously attempting to make known through her acting the idealized self which she sees in the private mirror of her own self-regard.

I remember one student who provided a particularly good example of the Narcissa complex. She was a plain girl with a dumpy figure and an unpleasant voice. She worked hard and was extremely critical of, and disliked by, her fellow students. No one would ever have suspected that she had ambitions to play anything but character parts. Through hard work she improved her voice, learned to move better, and then dyed her hair and began to use make-up and striking clothes. She was still without charm, and her rather unpleasant personality was never really very well disguised. Nevertheless she developed romantic and unrewarded passions for men who were much sought after and she confided to me that she knew she would be a great success as Juliet. This is an example of narcissism far outrunning any possibility of realization.

The female drama student never wants to play old or

ugly women unless the story is of an ugly duckling turning into a beautiful swan. Such a part has an intimate appeal because it may accord with the student's personal
drama. The world does not yet appreciate her, her fellow
students and her teachers may see her as an ugly, or at
least a commonplace, duckling. Yet when she gazes into
her private mirror, she can see a swan.

During her period of training the girl may also find that
her social life is pleasant as well as her home life. She is
probably quite a success socially because the traditional
glamour of the actress enhances her attractions. It is quite
possible that at this period of her life Narcissa will be happier than she will ever be again, whether the future brings
success or not. At drama school girls are, as a rule a great
deal happier than the boys. This is not only because the
boy may have encountered parental opposition to his career but because he usually has far more definite ideas
about exactly what he wants to do and how he wants to
do it. As a result he often finds himself in conflict with
his teachers' ideas. Serious psychological upsets or breakdowns are rare among girl students and less rare among
boys. If the girl has psychological difficulties during training these are more likely to be of the type that may beset
any girl—that is, an unrequited love or an unhappy love
affair.

It is only when Narcissa leaves her drama school that
she really encounters great difficulties. She is thrown into
the arduous competition of the theatrical dog fight for
survival. It is not surprising that many women students
leaving such schools marry within six months or a year
without ever having had a professional engagement. According to statistics on this subject at least fifty per cent
of the girl students who come from the drama schools

have given up the professional battle, married and retired within five years.

The intense overcrowding of the profession is not the only explanation of the high retirement rate among young actresses. The lives and careers of Duse and Ellen Terry, to mention two outstanding examples from the past, were continually seared and blasted by the exigencies of their private lives. They each left the stage for varying lengths of time and Ellen Terry did so for very long periods. These interludes did not operate unfavorably against them, because society believed that a woman's personal emotional life should rightfully take precedence over her career.

The private lives of Duse and Ellen Terry were almost as dramatic as their professional ones; on and off stage they existed in an aura of high romance. They knew that they were as much heroines in private as in public and to both of them this may have seemed natural and desirable. On the other hand an actor who abandoned his career again and again because of the demands of his sex life would lose caste both as an actor and as a man.

In modern times the stage actress is less spectacular as far as her private life is concerned. The private life of the film actress is more likely to be a source of sensational interest.

Because the actress begins as Narcissa does not mean that she cannot become a great artist. Emotional drives can be disciplined when they come into conflict with outside realities and indeed they have to be in the case of the modern actress. As the actress develops and matures she discards the mirror that first inspired her, a mirror which came between herself and reality but which, at the same time, helped to protect her from the harsher aspects of that reality when she would have flinched from them.

The process of development in the actress usually takes some years. She begins by discarding foibles accumulated in adolescence, foibles which were a form of defiance. She no longer makes a cult of certain styles, certain colors, acquired in drama student days. She no longer finds it necessary to talk at the top of her voice in public so that everyone will know she is an actress. She modifies irrational, and frequently spectacular, likes and dislikes. Defiance is replaced by a quiet poise.

The next step is more difficult and a great many actresses find it beyond them. It is to abandon narcissistic trends and personal fantasies, and to direct their psychic energy into their stage performances instead of wasting it on personal dramas in their private lives. It often means giving up a cherished idea, held by many young actresses, that they have within them the secret power of deciphering the souls of others. So often one may hear the young actress say, "I know exactly the sort of parts So-and-So should play but he [or she] does not realize it." Also the young actress has to try and stop believing in her own sexual uniqueness. She should not say—or think—that she has some peculiar ability to play love scenes more convincingly than anyone else. These beliefs not only give an actress false notions about her own abilities but they are likely to make her unpopular with her professional associates. Time and experience help to bring about changes of attitude and that is one reason why actresses need more time than actors to reach maturity.

There are signs, however, that this process may become less lengthy. Both economic conditions and education are playing a part in helping women toward development as individuals. Many more women both unmarried and married seek a living away from home. It is now easy for them to do so and in many cases they are employed and trained

at the same time. In the case of the girl with acting aspirations this is very valuable.

Girls usually develop their acting ambitions while they
are still at school. In the past, parents were confronted
with the problem that if a daughter was to work, training
of some sort had to be paid for before she could do so.
If a schoolgirl daughter was set on becoming an actress it
often happened that the parents would decide that they
would give her a chance by spending the money set aside
for her on her dramatic training. If the girl did not make
good she was then thrown on the ordinary labor market
untrained in any way that would enable her to earn a
good living. I knew one girl who, although she did well
at drama school, was not psychologically suited to a career
as an actress. She never obtained an engagement. Faced
with the need to earn a living, she eventually had to work
as an office cleaner because her parents could do no more
for her. Today such a girl could obtain a much better
type of employment and be trained while working so that
she could continue to make progress in her job.

Another point is that a very young girl who has just left
school and who believes she wants to be an actress would
often do better to first of all seek some ordinary job and
work at it for a few years. If, at the end of that time, she
still wishes to become a drama student she can do so. Her
experiences in the outside world will have been of great
benefit to her. If she has, in the meanwhile, abandoned
her ambitions to become an actress, then she will have no
regrets and will not have gone through the heartbreaking
process of failing in the theatre after spending several
years in a drama school.

If she finds that she experiences greater happiness and
satisfaction in her private rather than in her professional
life she may come to accept the fact that the stage at-

tracted her for reasons that have little to do with art. She may discover that she has been struggling to assert her right to act just to show the world and her parents that she is a person with a will of her own. She can then leave the theatre to those who have a fanatical sense of dedication to acting. Such women either have no sense of loss in foregoing some of the pleasures other women take for granted or they have so much strength of character and energy that they manage to get a satisfactory balance between their careers as actresses and their private lives. To do this demands very unusual qualities, because in all realms of theatrical entertainment there is far more hard work and far less leisure for the actress than in the past. To become a success—and remain a success—the actress has to keep herself constantly before the public.

The young actress who determines to struggle on, to resolve her own inner conflict between woman and artist, must cling to the knowledge that art is long and that life while short is also full of changes. No one wants to alienate herself from the society in which she lives, but social prejudices, customs and attitudes are changing. It is not always the most enlightened sections of society that loudly express their opinions—often the ignorant are the most vociferous. The voice of the spirit is not the loudest; it may be a still, small voice which tells the young woman that she too has the right to be an individual and an artist.

CHAPTER ten

THE PSYCHOLOGY OF THE AMATEUR

In the days of Charles Dickens amateur actors performed in booths and paid to do so on a scale regulated by the importance of their roles. The amateur who aspired to playing Hamlet might pay as much as ten shillings for the privilege, while he who was content with a tiny part might satisfy his ambition for as little as sixpence.

Nowadays amateurs in Great Britain fall into several groups and in the United States into an even larger number of groups. The most publicized amateur company in Great Britain is the Oxford University Dramatic Society from which it is not unusual for a player to step onto the West End stage without further ado, or for a producer to get an engagement in professional theatre. Naturally this very exclusive society has advantages, social and financial, denied to other groups. Most universities have amateur dramatics of some sort but those concerned have neither the facilities nor the status accorded to corresponding university-theatre activities in the United States where, although the level of acting may not be higher, the mechanical and technical aids and equipment compare favorably with those in professional theatres.

In the United States, university education per head of the population is greater than in Britain, where it is much more usual for the would-be professional actor to enter a full-time drama school at the age of seventeen or eighteen rather than to go to a university. Among those who do go to a university there may be some enthusiastic amateur actors, but their professional responsibilities seldom permit them to continue with amateur acting once they leave the university.

The amateur who wishes to have training in acting after the age of seventeen, and who has the leisure to attend evening classes, can do so at an evening institute if there is one in his vicinity. Educational authorities who have helped to make dramatic training a part of adult education were not mainly interested in the standard of performance achieved. Their main interest was to enable large numbers of young people to benefit from the cultural influence of dramatic training. The standard of teaching is becoming increasingly higher, however, and many of the teachers are on the staffs of the full-time drama schools. This means that a talented student at an evening institute can obtain a complete course of training if he or she wishes to take up a professional career, and a small number do so. Sometimes a student may—after some training in evening classes—seek an audition for a scholarship at a full-time drama school and win it.

The majority of students who come to evening classes are not doing so because they have definite plans for a career on the stage. Although many of them may envy the

successful professional actor they have no desire to undertake the hard work, training and struggle of the actor's
early years. At the same time they do believe in the need
for training if they are to act in amateur productions.
They also get a great deal of satisfaction out of the fact
that their teachers and producers in the evening institutes
have a professional background and qualifications, and
that class productions are therefore of an efficient standard as a rule.

Apart from the small number of amateurs who seek tui-
tion there are thousands who receive little training or no
training at all. There are many business firms that or-
ganize drama groups among their employees, subsidize
productions so that they can be lavishly staged in a theatre,
and employ a professional producer. The producer will do
what training is possible during the months of production.
The bulk of the amateur movement, however, is exactly
what the layman imagines the phrase to mean; that is, untrained players working under an amateur producer. Some
of these groups are ambitious and have their own theatres
but the majority do not.

The one thing amateur actors have in common with the
professional is the desire to have a little world of their
own where they can get away from "the dullness of ordinary life." They usually have occupations which do not
give them much opportunity for self-expression, and
which do not absorb them mentally. People with more
demanding and absorbing occupations may be attracted
to amateur acting for a while but they usually find after
a time that they have neither the energy nor the leisure
to devote to acting. Of course the majority of amateur
actors become interested, in their late teens or early twenties, and as they get older both their work and their private
lives demand more of their time and more of their inter-

est. With adolescence behind them they gradually become adjusted to their everyday lives. In a great many cases their everyday lives have become richer as a result of their acting experience. The young people who are attracted to amateur acting in the first place are likely to have more vitality, alertness and intelligence than their fellows. Acting helps to kindle their imaginations, improves their speech and movement and gives them poise. The confidence acquired through public appearances is a further asset. All this adds to their chances of advancement in their jobs and greater responsibility, and in this way many good actors are lost to the amateur stage. Naturally the students in evening class are even more affected by this factor than those working in purely amateur societies and as a result it is not easy to keep a group of students intact for more than a couple of years.

I was able to carry out a survey among drama students at literary institutes; the results differed in an interesting way from those obtained from full-time students or professional players. This was not possible among purely amateur groups but I have had opportunities of observing and listening to these.

As with most people, the primary desire of the amateur is to have what fun he can. Nevertheless, the emotional drives toward being the center of attention, the monarch in a tiny kingdom, must be present in some degree in the amateur actor just as the narcissistic tendency, innate in all women, must operate a little more strongly among amateur actresses. At the same time, the strongest impulse that inspires the amateur actor, whether he is a trained student or not, is the desire for some group effort unconnected with home or family, daily occupation or material gain. He is not a frustrated professional; he is not sufficiently uncomfortable emotionally to need to be one.

It might be supposed that the amateur actor would be a strong supporter of the professional theatre. In fact, apart from those who seek training in literary institutes, he is likely to go to the theatre far less frequently than many people who do not profess to take any particular interest in drama. The most direct help the British amateur gives the professional theatre is in the enormous royalties paid to playwrights, many of whom live comfortably on these without ever having one of their plays performed by a professional company. There are two reasons why the amateur actor is not a great playgoer. One is that he wants to participate in a play to a greater extent than is possible for a member of an audience, and secondly because the really keen amateur actor is unlikely to have much leisure time for anything apart from this hobby. That there is great satisfaction to be obtained from amateur acting seems to be confirmed by the fact that there are about thirty thousand amateur dramatic societies in Great Britain with a total of half a million members.

The standard of achievement in these societies is not always high, the actors may not succeed in moving their audiences, but all the same, as with the child who succeeds in attracting and holding attention, the amateur actor gets pleasure from his performances. The narrower and less colorful his previous existence has been the greater the satisfaction he gets from appearing on a stage.

In his first attempts as an actor the amateur is not only unaware of the hard facts of acting but is unwilling to accept them. If the subject is discussed he is likely to fall back on the cliché that acting ability must be a "gift." He has never realized that acting (apart from the learning of lines) is hard work, and sincerely believes that the professional is born with some peculiar ability which enables him to become an actor without any special effort. If his only contact with professional actors and their work has been as a member of an audience his illusion is excusable, since the more finished a performance the more effortless it appears to be.

Once the stimulating effect of having made a public appearance has worn off, the amateur may feel that his acting had many defects and to believe that acting is a "gift" will salve his pride. If he continues to study and work he will learn to develop his ability and acquire more confidence. Even if he never becomes outstanding the psychological benefits the amateur derives from acting may be considerable. While adjudicating at an amateur drama festival I was impressed by the performance of a middle-aged man, who later informed me that he had taken up acting in an attempt to cure a very bad stammer. In this he had been completely successful.

Another student, a boy of eighteen, came to a class of mine because he was handicapped by excessive shyness. He scarcely spoke above a whisper and shambled rather than walked, with shoulders hunched. His speech and carriage improved within a few weeks. He told me that he had felt very isolated and that he had little in common with other people. He also complained about "the dullness of ordinary life and work." After a few months he decided that he wanted to become a professional actor and he developed a good deal of self-assurance and the germ of acting ability. After a year he entered for a scholarship to a full-time dramatic school and won it.

Most youngsters who come for training in evening classes are shy, inaudible and awkward in movement. They are often untidy or dowdy in dress and careless in grooming. Gradually their appearance changes along with their speech and carriage: they become smart and well groomed. They also develop self-confidence, affability and ease of manner. Acting develops and invigorates the whole personality.

It may be asked, "What has therapeutic benefit to the individual to do with art?" "Art," I heard a celebrated actress say on the radio, "is not a bottle of medicine." Neither, however, is art of any kind an abstract force. All artistic impulses spring from man's unconscious, which has not only atavistic but spiritual energies. The tremendous artistic impulse in man is what distinguishes him from other creatures. Because this creative impulse is so deep, it cannot help affecting the whole personality just as a spring of water affects the soil around it. All expression of artistic impulse, however faulty and inept it may be, enriches the personality, just as the suppression or frustration of artistic impulse impoverishes the personality. The public is, to some extent, conscious of the benefits it gains from watching a play. Yet neither the public nor the professional actor is aware of the psychological benefits acting confers on the actor himself. The amateur actor or part-time student is usually more alive to the therapeutic effect of training and acting.

Such a student often comes from a drab background and his acting class is a magic casement which enables him to obtain a new concept of his own life and the world around him. He learns that to be articulate about all sorts of ideas and impressions is neither "daft" nor "soppy" but natural and stimulating. His acting may never add much to the histrionic art of his time but it sets him free from many of the social and cultural handicaps which may imprison him in a narrow and frustrating environment.

For success in any occupation the individual has to feel that he can do what he desires as well as, if not better than, other people. On the whole this kind of confidence is only engendered by a fair social background and a reasonably good education. For those who lack these assets amateur acting can be of very great help.

Among students in evening classes in working-class areas I have found a deep conviction that they will never get a fair chance if they desire to break away from their social and working environment. They are still the victims of prejudices and ideas that belong to a bad old British tradition. They do not realize that many professional men, including actors, have come from families no better off financially than they are themselves. It had not occurred to any of them to cross the line from "East" to "West" in order to visit a West End theatre. Nor had it occurred to those living on the north bank of the Thames to cross over the river to visit the Old Vic Theatre. When I suggested to some of them that they should do this they did not even know what transport would take them there. Many of them had never seen a performance in a "live" theatre, to them acting meant film acting. The awe and delight newcomers in this class expressed when one of the more experienced members of the class got up on the stage for rehearsal was both revealing and pathetic. I remember one boy saying to me, "I can't get over it. There was old So-and-So talking to me about something ordinary and the next minute he got up there and became somebody else. Do you really think I shall ever be able to do that?" Hidden under an unprepossessing exterior this boy had real talent and imagination. Two months later he was up on the stage and he too was able to be "somebody else" for a few minutes. "Maybe it's because I had an Irish grandmother," he told me.

There was some truth in this remark. The "Cockney" may be almost aggressively proud of his origin yet he has inferiority feelings about it and about his accent. Less

ignominy attaches to other dialects and the Welsh, Irish
and Scots find that their brogues are much liked. Teachers
in drama schools or in evening classes can tackle the problem of these brogues with nothing but the utmost good
feeling from all concerned but one has to exercise great
diplomacy when seeking to eradicate a Cockney accent in
a student.

Although efforts have been made by educational authorities to make drama classes and performances by amateurs available to young people living in the East End of
London, the fight has been an uphill one. The less favorable the social situation of a person the less able he is to
work hard at some pastime, however much he may be
attracted to it. Acting demands concentration and above
all initiative. Initiative is what the underprivileged person
so often lacks. Where a concrete and obvious idea or ideal
is put before him, he does better. For instance Unity
Theatre has had outstanding amateur actors, many of
whom came from the East End. Their political ideals
gave them the confidence needed to build up a theatre
movement.

A similar theatre movement created the Dublin Abbey
Theatre. Headed by W. B. Yeats, a group of middle-class
idealists who believed that a theatre could be a torch for
Ireland's political freedom recruited amateur players from
factories, workshops and offices. All were able to rally
round something well within their comprehension, a
patriotic ideal. These players did have the great advantage
that their plays were written for them so their brogues
were no handicap. The Abbey Theatre is unique in that
plays written by amateurs for amateurs created the link
between an amateur theatre and the professional theatre.

In England a number of playwrights have come from
the ranks of amateur actors and had their first plays per-

formed by members of the dramatic societies to which they belonged. Unfortunately, in nearly all cases, once such playwrights obtained any recognition they firmly attached their wagon to the star of commercial theatre. Usually they have done so not only because this made their plays more profitable but because they lacked the knowledge or insight to wish to write any other type of play. From every point of view amateur theatre in England has increased in size rather than in stature. It has certainly proved to be of psychological benefit to those who act in it and in doing so fully justifies its existence even though it has contributed little or nothing to theatrical art as a whole.

It seems possible that there will be an improvement as far as the achievements of the amateur theatre are concerned. Shorter working hours are already giving amateurs more time and energy to devote to their pastime. At present the lead is coming from the trained students in the evening institute classes, and has taken place as a result of something that seemed a severe setback. This is not unusual in theatre of any kind that is either manned by professionals or led by a professional. The teacher-producers in these evening institutes are nearly all professionals.

The organization of these classes is along lines which run counter to those usual in organized education. A class is announced in the syllabus and a teacher is engaged for the season. The students enrolling pay what is practically a token fee but unless at least fifteen have enrolled within three weeks of the start of the class, then the class is closed. The teacher loses the engagement and the students lose the fees they have paid unless they can be transferred to another class in the same subject or—if this is not available —to a class in a completely different subject.

The great increase in earnings which took a sharp upward movement in Great Britain in the early fifties, together with paid holidays, turned the attention of many young people to foreign travel. This meant a new interest in foreign languages. The demand for language classes soared and there was a corresponding drop in the demand for other classes, including drama.

In order to combat the disaster (drama classes were reduced by at least one-third) the teachers took action. Through advertising and personal contacts they reached people of all ages who were interested in learning to act and arranged for these people to become students in the evening classes. The more enterprising of these teacher-producers have now created groups with a far stronger team spirit—and far more potential talent—than existed previously. In addition to paying their fees these students are willing to make small contributions toward better presentations of the plays and it is not unusual for small theatres to be hired for performances in cases where the premises provided by the institute are not satisfactory.

These are hopeful signs and foundations may be laid for a kind of community theatre somewhat on the lines of those familiar in the United States. The players would enjoy the added advantage, of course, that they would not only be working under professional producers but would be receiving full training in speech and acting technique.

CHAPTER eleven

PSYCHIC HANDICAPS

There is a popular illusion that the amateur actor performs for sheer love of the theatre and the professional actor for money and fame. This is not so. What is done in any art has its roots in self-love, love of the art comes later. Self-love must come first because no one who hates, dislikes or despises himself can be a great artist, he can only be a frustrated and psychically crippled person. The small boy who becomes the center of attention by using his charm and talent must believe that he is the possessor of these attributes; in other words, he must have self-love and self-esteem. In the same way the girl who is Narcissa must believe that she has qualities that will enable her to make a favorable impression on people, and she must have them to a degree likely to influence her future career.

Usually it is only after contact has been made with the stern realities of the theatre that the embryo actor or actress becomes aware of the possibilities of failure.

It is not always easy to predict the future of a young

118

player. Usually it is some years before an immature actor masters the technique of acting. In the beginning he is its slave. This period of slavery is, however, a necessary apprenticeship and without it the player may remain an amateur completely at the mercy of his own emotions. Only a stalwart individual can ever get beyond this phase, for acquiring technique is a formidable task and assimilating it a demanding process.

Since chance must influence opportunity it is not realistic to make a list of certain qualities and arrive at the conclusion that those possessing them can become successful actors. There may be factors in personality or environment that will undermine progress and achievement.

Replies to my questionnaire revealed that most actors came from families with several children. Few successful actors are only children but a large number of actresses are. This may be because only children are unused to competition in the family circle and are therefore unlikely to survive in the most highly competitive of all professions. It is slightly easier for a girl to do so because her inner confidence rests in what she is, or what she believes herself to be, rather than in what she does. It is the boy who has to prove himself in action.

A study of the background of some well-known theatrical figures reveals that a significantly large number of playwrights, producers and stage designers were only children, or, through some chance in the family structure, occupied the position usually held by an only child. The only child is very likely to be an individualist and a lonely person; he may long to be part of a group, but he gets along better by working on his own or by controlling others.

In some ways the only child has advantages over the sibling, particularly in the material field. He may get a better education and have a higher standard of life and comfort than the member of a large family. This is favorable to his physical and mental development but may not be altogether beneficial emotionally. Many only children never succeed in emancipating themselves from undue, even if benevolent, parental influence. Those who do break away are inclined to be so wary of authority that they are never at ease in working under others but only when they themselves have power, at least over their own work or development.

This inability to work happily under the direction of others can sometimes be a real handicap, as it was in the case of an only child whom I shall call Basil. Basil's childhood seemed so delightful to him that the boy had no incentive to grow up either mentally or emotionally, but he did want to become King of the Castle in the outside world just as he was in his home. His background was prosperous but uncultured. Because he was a very pretty child and lively he was petted and indulged not only by his parents, but by other relatives. He sang and danced from an early age and was sent to a children's class for these subjects. Soon he began to appear in children's shows, first near his home but gradually farther and farther away. His mother liked traveling around with the child and life was a succession of rehearsals, appearances, parties and moving from place to place. "I had no real education because we traveled about so much that I was allowed to do as I pleased," Basil wrote of his childhood.

Because the boy did not see his father often, little discipline was imposed and there was less when his father died at an early age. There was not so much money now but relatives were still generous. When he was fifteen years old Basil was sent to a well-known school; he was far behind his classmates and was so self-willed and unused to discpline that his masters could do nothing with him. Then the war broke out and Basil persuaded his mother to allow him to leave school and get a job in a theatre. Since there was a great demand for youths not yet due for conscription Basil had no difficulty in obtaining work. Ill-equipped, he stepped confidently into a kingdom he regarded as his own. Confidence soon gave way to an aggressive cocksureness that hid bewilderment. An extraordinary degree of exhibitionism combined with such elementary knowledge of theatre craft as he had picked up as a child singer and dancer were far from enough to enable him to be a successful actor.

Several years later Basil was conscripted, but was so unsuited to the discipline of the Army that those responsible for him seem to have been glad to direct him into Army Entertainments so that he was never in combat. After demobilization, Basil assumed that he would immediately find a place in the theatre. He soon discovered that it was impossible for a man in his twenties, with little education and no proper training in drama, to find work. The only realm in which he might have got a toehold—musical comedy—he now considered unworthy of his talents.

Had he been more modest, Basil might have obtained poorly paid work as a beginner in straight drama but, always having lived in a certain amount of luxury, he was not prepared to endure poverty. He was enraged by the progress of others who had never stepped on a stage until they were adult, but who had gone through what Basil considered the dreary treadmill of a normal education followed by a couple of years' hard study in a dramatic school.

Also, no matter where Basil worked, he was still too intolerant of discipline to accept it. After a few years he decided that he would become a producer. This would allow him to direct other people and to be independent. He scarcely knew the name of a serious play or of a classic playwright and was completely ignorant of dramatic literature, so he found that he could not command the respect of trained actors or technicians.

With the passing of time Basil's career has been so undistinguished that he frequently threatens to leave the theatre altogether. He cannot understand why he should stay where he is not appreciated and where he cannot earn enough to enjoy the extravagant existence he had as a child-performer.

Psychologically Basil is still a child and likely to remain one. In turn charming, sulky, hysterically bad tempered, a fantastic exhibitionist and fanatically jealous of anyone else's success, however modest, Basil is regarded by most men with active dislike and with good-humored contempt by women. Every part of Basil's early life made him unfit for a serious and demanding profession and at the same time it was almost inevitable that he should regard a successful theatrical career as his natural right.

While Basil is an example of the failure of an indulged only child in the theatre, John's experiences were very different. His background was less materially prosperous than that of Basil but less uncultured because his mother had romantic yearnings toward art. Dissatisfied with her marriage to a mediocre businessman, the mother eloped with a handsome young actor, taking her baby son with her.

The following years were marked by emotional tension and by money troubles. Sometimes the mother and child followed the actor on tour, more often they remained behind in lodgings. At length the liaison petered out.

Deprived of a secure background or settled family relationships, John withdrew into himself. He was a lonely child with a tendency to daydreams and a vague love of poetry. The feeling that without him his mother's life might have been less difficult and overshadowed, as he had been by the dynamic and charming personality of her lover, John had a haunting sense of inferiority. He had no great interests and no special abilities. When the time came for him to earn a living he was not sure what he wanted to do.

To the mother it seemed inevitable that her son should go on the stage. She had long fostered the ambition that he should become a great actor. Yet she had never tried to obtain any real training for him and he had little in the way of looks or personality to recommend him. Nevertheless, the mother prevailed upon her old lover to get the boy a start in the theatre.

Because of John's history the other players in the company made extraordinary efforts to help. They taught him all they could, were indulgent of his inadequacies and generally carried him along. Then the outbreak of war brought opportunities that might never have occurred in normal times. In due course he found himself playing a leading role in a famous London theatre.

Sensitive, still suffering from inferiority feelings and aware of his own limitations and technical ignorance, John was almost completely lacking in confidence. That he should be regarded as an adult, expected to make important decisions and be carrying a part in a famous play with all the responsibilities this involved, unnerved him still further. Nothing seemed quite real, nothing seemed safe. Then John made the discovery that alcohol had the power to reassure him and lift him out of his depression.

A short time after the run of his play began he was found to be hopelessly intoxicated just before curtain time. John was dismissed and with this dismissal his career was ended, at least as far as any West End parts were concerned.

He lapsed into obscurity, got occasional provincial engagements and continued drinking. Eventually he met and married a strong-minded young woman who controlled and directed his behavior in the way his mother had done. Since then he has cut down on his drinking or even refrained from it altogether and manages to earn a fair living by acting. It might seem that to do this is sufficient reward, but no young actor entering the theatre sees himself as a fair success but as a great actor. In many cases he gradually adjusts himself to being less than great and leads a rewarding and satisfactory life, but this is not so in John's case, for several reasons. First of all because of his mother's romantic dream of him as a great actor—greater than the lover to whom she gave so much. Also, the fact that he nearly attained great fame and lost it through his own fault has had a lasting psychological effect. John's brief outburst of bonhomie never returned and he remains a withdrawn and frustrated personality.

The whole pattern of this actor's life gives a picture of what can happen when a not particularly intelligent child, who lacks many of the qualities needed for great success, drifts toward or is directed into a profession for which his personal disposition is not really suited.

The type of person who prefers to spend much of his time alone, and who finds continuous association with others irritating, can seldom hope to make a great success and can never hope to be really at ease in the gregarious life of the theatre. There are notable exceptions and perhaps the best known is Henry Irving, who was both an only child and a naturally seclusive personality. Irving overcame his handicap because he was disciplined from the earliest age by his parents' moral and social attitudes and by poverty. He was able to endure hardship and struggle against difficulties of all kinds.

Henry Broadribb, who became known as Henry Irving, was born into the rigidly respectable home of a small provincial shopkeeper. When this business failed, the family moved to London and occupied rooms over city offices, where it is said the mother acted as caretaker. The boy's schooling was the parents' constant preoccupation and they made sacrifices to give him as good an education as they could afford. Nevertheless, soon after his thirteenth birthday young Henry went out to work as an office boy.

Even the long working hours of those days did not deter the boy from joining an evening class for elocution and dramatic study, nor from becoming an outstanding pupil.

High ideals and hard work were the keystones in the career of one who seemed to have little natural fitness, either physically or temperamentally, for a career in the theatre. In the beginning he was very unsuccessful and made a most unfavorable impression upon his audiences. Partly because of this he was paid no salary but existed on his meager savings. A little later he was paid twenty-five shillings a week, out of which he helped his parents. This left him no money for shoe repairs or even an overcoat. Despite these hardships, the actor never swerved from the course which he had set himself. It was some years before he made good and it was his single-minded determination, his thrift, and his extraordinary self-discipline that carried him to fame.

It is significant, considering that Irving was an only child, that his greatest success did not come until he was an actor-manager and responsible only to himself. He had considerable business ability and there can be little doubt that this contributed to his success. He had few of the character traits usually to be found in the actor. He never shared his thoughts with anyone, he had no natural social talents and small gift for friendship. He seemed to give out light rather than warmth and many of those who offered him love seem to have been hurt because he appeared to have no need of it. His audiences knew little of his private life, which was so obscure that even when his marriage of only two years foundered and later ended in divorce, few people knew about it. His behavior was so correct that divorce, a scandal of first magnitude in Irving's early days, seems to have left him publicly unscathed. Even old actors who knew Irving in their youth are surprised to learn—or to recall—that he was divorced.

It is interesting to speculate on what the career of Henry Irving might have been if he had been born at a later date. He started his career in the era of the actor-manager and it must be remembered that this was a period when the modern producer, or director as he is now called, did not exist in his own right. The actor-manager directed his own productions. Irving was one of the first of the great men of the theatre to criticize the carelessness in production and over-all planning that he found in the theatre of his youth. His own hard work as a manager and a director far surpassed that of his predecessors. He raised the whole standard of theatrical art to greater heights. It seems very possible that he was the source of inspiration for Gordon Craig's vision of a theatre that would offer a unity of all the arts needed for first-class productions. Craig failed in his efforts to do this because he lacked the qualities necessary for such a gigantic task. If Irving had been thirty years younger he might have found fame as a director rather than an actor and psychologically this might have given him greater serenity and satisfaction.

Another only child who became a famous actor, Edmund Kean, had some of the characteristics of Basil, John, and Henry Irving. Like Basil, Kean was naturally charming as a child and good-looking. He too was a spoiled child to some extent because of his precocious talent. What he did lack was any stability in his background. He was an illegitimate child brought up in the mean streets around Drury Lane and cared for by a minor actress. His childhood was sordid and desperately insecure. He lacked formal education and was ever intolerant of discipline. From an early age he had a fanatical desire to achieve something that would give him the status denied to him at birth. He fought for what he wanted like a fierce little wolf cub. Like John he bolstered up his courage with alcohol in later years. Alcoholism is tolerated today in the theatre only for as long as the offender can still give a good performance, but once he is incapable of fulfilling this obligation his career will not continue for long. Kean was not only intoxicated on stage on many occasions but often too drunk to make his way to the theatre. Yet the only time a penalty was inflicted upon him was when he was barred from the London theatre for some months.

When sober, Kean was dour and unsociable. When drunk he was convivial and wild in his behavior. With the passing of time he become more and more of a recluse.

The actor who cannot get along with other people may strive in many ways to build up a defense against his poor adjustment to human relationships. Irving did this by a fanatical devotion to the theatre, but this did not completely solve his problem. All those who were in closest contact with him seem agreed that he lacked emotional warmth in his personal relationships. A very old actor who knew him in the last years of his career told me that he was withdrawn and melancholy.

The great actor cannot dissipate his energies in social life without damaging his career. It is his inner feelings in regard to other people that are important. Basil quarreled with other people because they realized his limitations and he refused to do so. John had secret feelings of inferiority and could only feel at ease with others when he drank with them. Kean was at war with society because of his early life. Unless he was drunk he could not endure other people.

The actor who is unable to have successful relationships with others should try to realize that the difficulties may arise through his own attitude to his fellow human beings rather than to defects in them or in their attitude to him.

Overanxiety in regard to his own success is another handicap that affects the actor and it is one that afflicts most actors in some degree. I have not carried out an extensive analysis of the dreams of actors but where I have done so there has often been a great similarity in the dream content. The setting of the dreams is usually either on a stage or backstage of a theatre. It is scarcely necessary to say that when on stage the dreamer is the central or even the sole player. Sometimes he is scoring a fantastic triumph but it is marred by some untoward happening. This is often the dream of a young actor. The successful actor may have a dream about playing a leading role and forgetting his lines. If the dreamer is backstage he may discover that at the very moment he is about to make his entrance some other famous actor has suddenly strode on and taken his place. As a contrast, a struggling actor told me of a dream he had in which Sir Laurence Olivier and John Barrymore were enacting a scene and he walked on and began to act with them.

All these dreams make it obvious that the actor's profession possesses not only his conscious but his unconscious mind. All are what is called anxiety dreams, the anxiety of the young actor to make good, the haunting anxiety of the successful actor to remain a success. This type of dream is common not only to the real artist who is able to give a fine portrayal of a part but to the more superficial player who can only give a performance.

CHAPTER twelve

INTROVERTS AND
EXTROVERTS

The terms "extrovert" and "introvert" are convenient for reference but not very many people are completely extrovert or introvert. If they were, their behavior would probably be rather eccentric. Many members of the public imagine that actors must be extroverts and will refer to some notorious characters whose names are always in the news. Such people seldom enjoy—or deserve—lasting success. The playboy star is a thing of the past. On the other hand the introvert is unlikely to be happy in the world of the theatre of today.

The players who answered my questionnaire did not seem to be extroverts. The pastimes and interests they had would have been unlikely to serve as material for sensational publicity. Of course these were the kind of people who were most likely to answer the questionnaire. I also made a point of asking a group of my own students to answer the questionnaire, however, and one fact came to light which was interesting. It was two students who were unusually extrovert, people who were always trying to draw attention to themselves, who were least willing to answer the questions. It seemed that their customary behavior was based not on a real self-confidence but on the lack of it.

It is true that most actors prefer talking about themselves to any other topic, but this is not simply an indication of extroversion. In the theatrical profession the individual who is not buoyed up by the conviction that he is a most interesting person with unique talent and genius is more likely to sink than to swim. So egotism has to be tolerated and is indeed taken for granted. Even "putting on an act" may be accepted as an occupational necessity. One celebrated star does this when being interviewed by the press, with whom he is very popular. Having provided them with good copy he will suddenly relax and then say, "Well, boys, if you have all the guff you want let's have a drink." In fact the private life of the star is more like that of an introvert than of the extrovert the public imagines him to be. He has said more than once that he really prefers his own company and to a very great extent this is so.

As a contrast to this there is the star who needs an entourage of hangers-on to surround him with a comforting atmosphere of flattery. He can scarcely bear to be alone and is so preoccupied with the impression he makes that he fritters away time, energy and money. He may even loan or give away large sums of money in order to win a reputation for good nature and generosity. Such a type is a natural introvert who outrages his own innate tendencies in order to try to ease deep fears and anxieties but never really succeeds.

Scarcely less pitiable is the actor who needs alcohol to give him the confidence he does not otherwise possess. This type may be—and often is—a great artist. He is an introverted character who expects too much of himself and of others and is oversensitive to the hard knocks and the disappointments that are inevitable in the struggle for existence. Success cannot give him confidence. He is like somebody climbing a high tower who becomes more nervous the nearer he gets to the top. This is confirmed by the fact that alcoholism is not a problem among drama students or young actors. The actor who is addicted to alcohol is practically always somebody who has achieved success.

In some cases where success has been too sudden a naturally introverted character may become even more complex. This was what happened to Tom, who was born in a remote village far from any theatre. The family moved to a large city while the boy was very young and he became a typical child of his environment, intelligent, vital and charming. Then Tom's mother died and Tom was sent back to his grandmother in the village. The child hated and resented this and felt he was being punished for something he had not done. He missed his mother and all that she stood for. He came to dislike all old people, associating them with death, unhappiness and drabness.

For years the boy had nothing but visits to the movies to satisfy his nostalgic yearning for the past. He became introverted and solitary. At the same time he developed a fervid imagination, and a deep interest in poetry and the occult.

In his early teens Tom became an amateur actor. Later on he was seen by a leading actor in a touring company in a town some distance from his home, a homosexual who was attracted by his appearance. Tom was offered an engagement in the company and left home forever. His later career has alternated between unusual success and long periods of unemployment for which his temperament is responsible. He swings between depression, when he shuts himself away from everyone, and elation, when he seeks out a few intimate friends and is extremely voluble. In order to combat his shyness and oversensitivity he resorts to alcohol. He is unhappy inside the world of the theatre and even more unhappy outside it.

A number of friends and well-wishers have made efforts to win Tom away from his seclusion but with no success. Without a new emotional attitude to the world and more self-knowledge, he can make no real progress.

Another actor, who was a famous Shakespearean clown, was a tragic example of an introvert who could not be reassured by success. Alcoholism eventually led to his retirement. He died in a squalid room, a half-demented alcoholic.

It is futile for the individual who is of an introverted disposition to try to change his behavior instead of developing a different emotional attitude to life. This is exemplified in the history of another actor, whom we shall call Ralph. Here is his story in his own words:

My parents were bright young things in the twenties and they spent the rest of their lives in sackcloth and ashes as a result. I can scarcely ever remember my father laughing or my mother not looking anxious. My father was a soldier and it never occurred to him that I would not be a soldier also. From an early age I only heard two things discussed. One, our finances—my father had run through a large fortune when young and there was little left. The other topic was the Army, including my future as a soldier.

I was a puny youngster and in no way brave. The thought

of a future in the Army and of trying to live up to what Father expected was a nightmare to me, I hated prep school but it was worse when I went to a public school for the sons of "officers and gentlemen." I did badly.

Ralph never entered Sandhurst and eventually drifted into a little theatre group. He began to think that the theatre would provide him with exactly the kind of life he wanted. He was a bad mixer, however, and in order to keep up with the others he deliberately developed an extroverted type of behavior which eventually bordered on exhibitionism. He might have become a good actor if he had accepted his own introverted tendencies without trying to overcompensate for these trends by exhibitionism and the conflicts this engendered in him. He remained an isolated and displaced personality who really feared his audiences and hid his fears behind bravado. He had a good stage presence, imagination, a real love of art and intelligence above the average, yet he lacked sympathetic understanding. Those who cannot come to terms with themselves can scarcely hope to understand others. Not even a successful beginning in the theatre could give Ralph the reassurance he needed and he gave up his stage career.

When an actor tends to exhibitionism it is seldom realized that he may not be a truly extroverted personality but in fact an introverted one. This is so even in the case of great comedians. Many are introverted rather than extroverted characters. Off stage they may be serious and even somewhat dull. Those who retain their status in the theatre often seem to work out a balance in their lives by cultivating hobbies that are quite humdrum. I know one celebrated comedian who loves to mend household objects such as broken furniture and broken clocks.

In other cases an actor who has many of the characteristics of the introvert satisfies this side of his nature
through work directly connected with the theatre. One of
the most gifted introverts I knew helped to make a great
success of a repertory theatre with which he was associated.
He played leading parts and in addition would often take
over the whole direction of one production and build sets
and arrange the lighting as well. Everyone in the company
predicted a brilliant future for this actor but unfortunately he is not yet well known. He was too introverted
to make successful contacts with others, disliked competing for parts and was never able to make a good impression on agents or at an audition. Yet he is a brilliant
all-round man of the theatre.

Success is not impossible for a man of this type. One of
our most famous stars is basically of this disposition. He
had even greater difficulties than the young actor mentioned who was most outstanding in drama school and in
repertory. The star was not, because his introversion made
him uncertain and awkward in his early stage work. He
had the good fortune to have some influential friends who
believed in him and he became successful without having
to outrage his basic feelings. He too satisfies the side of his
nature which needs expression apart from public appearances by producing plays for other people. He has never
sought publicity and it seems that he never will. No publicity agent has been allowed to publicize the house in
which he lives, the domestic pets he may or may not have,
the sort of car he prefers or where he goes for his holidays.
The public has no idea where he lives, whether he has a
cat, a dog or a car or if he ever takes a holiday.

The more extrovert actors would never wish to produce
plays in which they themselves do not appear and they are
only too willing to allow the more superficial aspects of

their private lives to be publicized. In fact, the really clever ones co-operate so successfully with their publicity agents that the general public is not aware that they are publicity seekers. It appears that rather against their inclinations they are dogged by eager reporters and photographers who insist on publicizing them. This is, of course, the very peak of clever showmanship.

The fact remains, however, that no actor should shun publicity but should see that he obtains a reasonable amount of it until such time as his work has resulted in firmly established success. But publicity costs money and during his early years the young actor is unlikely to have money to spare. So to a great extent he has to be his own publicity agent. The more extroverted he is the more he enjoys doing this, and he often succeeds in doing far more for himself than any publicity agent could do for him at that stage of his career. Unfortunately his abilities in this direction may far outrun his talents as an actor or his opportunities to display them. One of the most extroverted and least talented young actors I ever had the misfortune to present was an example of this. For some years one saw his name mentioned at frequent intervals, always in connection with something he was about to do. None of these projects seemed to materialize. There are, however, many young actors who deal with this matter of personal publicity more judiciously and it is helpful to their careers.

Good taste may be involved in the kind of publicity an actor seeks or permits, but it does not follow that to refuse publicity of all kinds is a mark of superiority. True, the extrovert is not oversensitive and his work may lack the delicate edge of that of a more sensitive player, but he often appeals to wider audiences and is enormously successful in certain roles.

The introverted actor may find personal publicity an ordeal. He is almost incapable of getting any for himself and if some comes to him by chance he is in a terrible state of anxiety because he thinks it may create a wrong impression or unfavorable comment. So it often happens that in the theatre the more extroverted character may come off better than the introvert. His early efforts to attract attention and obtain publicity may be crude, but if he has real ability as an actor little harm is done. As he earns more, a professional publicity expert will probably take over. Usually life and experience tone down the overexuberance of the extrovert and make him a better-balanced personality. The introvert can only improve his lot by realizing his own character trends and making a firm effort to change those that may impede his progress. If he does not do so there is a great danger that a really fine artist may remain unknown or insufficiently known so that a wide public is deprived of seeing him. The career of one of the very great actors of the past twenty-five years, the late F. J. McCormack, is an example of how an actor who instinctively avoids publicity may do himself a tragic injustice.

For thirty years McCormack worked in the Abbey Theatre for little more than a subsistence wage. He passed from juvenile leads to middle-aged character parts. He was unknown to the English stage and, in fact, unknown to all but Abbey Theatre goers and to such sections of the American public who saw the Abbey Players during their occasional tours of the United States. Even to his fellow players, McCormack remained little known except professionally. He came from his home to his dressing room and then to the wings to wait to go on. As he stood there, McCormack ceased to be and the character he was playing took over. If any of the other actors spoke to him, he seemed not to hear. He seldom joined in any social activities but divided his life between his home and the theatre.

It was only necessary to see McCormack to know that his solitude was due not to any fear or dislike of people but because he lived in the world of the imagination. He certainly did not lack awareness of others—this was confirmed by his genius as a character actor in later life. No one who was unobservant of the types Sean O'Casey wrote about in such plays as *Juno and the Paycock, The Shadow of a Gunman,* and other successes, could have given such magnificent performances in them. McCormack not only interpreted each character he played, he illuminated it, from Torvald in *A Doll's House* to Joxer in *Juno and the Paycock.*

When the film moguls discovered McCormack, no one who knew the actor's work was surprised at the result. In *Odd Man Out* he created such a sensation that his part was given greater footage than had been originally planned. For the first time in his life McCormack found international fame and substantial material reward. A few months later, in his early fifties, he was dead. Yet if, as a young man, he could have foreseen that he would be struck down on the threshold of fame, it is doubtful if he would have deviated from his self-dedicated path. If he had wanted to he could have forsaken the Abbey Theatre for the West End, Broadway or Hollywood, as many of the Abbey Theatre Players who wanted more recognition and more material reward felt impelled to do. McCormack never seriously considered this any more than he ever considered that he was hiding his light under a bushel. He was content with the parts he played in the Abbey Theatre for a salary that a greenhorn actor of today would despise, and he was playing there when he was stricken by a fatal illness.

It was only on the stage that McCormack seemed fully present and a dynamic personality. Off stage he never seemed quite of this world. There can be no doubt of his achievements as an actor. It is only to be regretted that owing to his disregard for publicity, his unawareness of its value, his public was so restricted. Many young actors who knew his work in the Abbey Theatre have benefited from it, but more might have done so if he had performed elsewhere as well. The English public also was deprived of the opportunity of seeing a player who should have a place among the truly great actors of the twentieth century.

Many oversensitive actors who are rather introverted are made unhappy by various aspects of life in the theatrical profession. They may say that they have ideals and find it difficult to work with others who do not share those ideals. They say they love the theatre for what it might be and despise it for what it is. They overlook the fact that no actor, whether a star or a humble player, is content with the theatre as it is. Those who give up the struggle and drop out of the profession are surprised to find that many things of which they disapprove are to be found to a far greater degree in other occupations. In any event, the introverted character will find difficulties wherever he goes, so if he feels he has anything to contribute to the theatre he should try to serve it.

CHAPTER thirteen

SELF-DISCIPLINE

A would-be actor, given to pestering well-known actors in private life, once remarked to me that he was amazed at the demeanor of many of these actors when off stage. While playing they seemed fiery and dynamic, when not playing they seemed almost colorless personalities. The contradiction is a measure of the extraordinary self-discipline such stars have achieved. They have succeeded in discarding everything that is detrimental or without value to their artistic success. What "self-expression" they do indulge in they relegate to the privacy of their own homes or their most intimate circle.

The actor, to be successful, must learn to say, "Is this going to help me to be a better actor?" Whether or not an actor loathes a certain agent, or detests a certain producer or manager, is not important. If he insults the agent he makes an enemy—he does not make the agent change his ways. To disagree violently with a certain producer or manager does not give him the chance to play the part which was at issue or to enact a particular scene as *he* thought it should be done. If he needles a fellow player for deficiencies, real or imaginary, he accomplishes nothing useful. He only creates bad feeling which may spread through the whole company, and I have known many actors who have spoiled their own chances of success through this kind of self-indulgence.

To curb the inclination to interfere with the work of others in any group effort calls for self-restraint. Perhaps an individual actor could make a better job of the script than the playwright has done. Possibly he may be a better director than the one in charge. It may be that he could improve the lighting plot if only he had a free hand. However, these things are not his concern.

Whenever the subject of self-discipline comes up it is inevitable that the name of one of the most undisciplined of past stars should be mentioned—John Barrymore. Under present-day conditions, however, not even an actor of such talent could repeat the Barrymore pattern of behavior. In any event, the unique psychological background that produced the individual who was John Barrymore could never occur again.

Even a very different type of self-indulgence such as was prevalent among some famous actor-managers up to the outbreak of the first World War would be impossible today. For instance, the actor-manager who chose plays irrespective of their merit so long as they offered a showy part for the star. The rest of the cast had little to do, the star did not care very much how they did it, and insufficient attention was paid to the production as a whole. Today such a star would find great difficulty in getting financial backing for his productions and, despite the unemployment in the theatre, difficulty in getting actors of any standing to become members of his cast.

The nearest approach to actor-managers of this type may sometimes be found in English repertory and they usually become the victims of their own unbridled egotism and lack of self-discipline. I know of one whose own eagerness for star parts often causes him to miss opportunities. In a modern play the longest part is not always the most theatrically effective part. Occasionally a player in a shorter part may "steal the thunder." After a season during which this happened on more than one occasion, the actor-manager announced that audiences seemed to be becoming so stupid that he was thinking of giving up acting altogether.

The passing of the costume drama so popular up to the first World War has also affected the completely selfish and self-centered star. In those days he was not only on the stage longer than anyone else but he could wear much more resplendent costumes, and a greater variety of costumes, than anyone else. This was a source of satisfaction to him—and of dissatisfaction to the rest of the cast. In the few modern costume plays there are, the greatest attention is paid to all the costumes because the producer is concerned with the stage picture as a whole and not just the appearance of one or two leading players.

The modern theatre is one of rules, red tape and big business. Power is not so completely one-sided as it was in the past. Trade-unionism is a force with which to reckon. For many reasons the modern actor tries to be a conformist in everything but the driving necessity to follow his instinct to act. In addition to all this, if he is a valuable box-office attraction, managements are likely to take great precautions to see that an actor is protected from his own weaknesses. An actor whose behavior deviates from the prevailing social code is likely to have guardians to see that he does not make a slip.

The change-over from the theatre of the actor-manager to the theatre of highly organized big business is not the only reason for the changed attitude to the actor with antisocial traits, even if he is a man of genius. Some knowledge of psychology is now available to everyone. In the past, moral yardsticks were the only means of assessing a man's behavior. He could be "good" or "bad," a near saint or a sinner. Today these terms would not be used except by very simple people. The transgressor is referred to as a neurotic, a maladjusted personality or a sick person. Drunkards are known as alcoholics and alcoholism is known to be a malady. The playboys of the Western world are explained as emotionally immature and there cannot be any glory or daredevil glamour in such a reputation. Society no longer wrings its hands and prays for its sinners—it is more likely to send them to a psychiatrist.

Yet society still has unconscious yearnings toward immature behavior and is fascinated by the social rebel, so long as his actions do not affect welfare and progress. That is why the screen hero of the present time is very primitive and the playwright scores successes with characters who are fighting a one-man war against accepted social standards. But in real life these characters would be called "confused" or "mixed-up kids." Such labels deflate even the most egotistic person.

It may be asked, "Has the actor no religious faith to help him to discipline himself?"

This is not easy to answer because the whole question of religious belief and, more important still, of the part such belief plays in everyday life is complex.

Only a small minority of actors are avowed atheists. Nearly all actors are aware of the sacred origins of their calling and that drama and religion have been linked since early days. Most actors, whatever religious ideas they may have, believe that acting has a strongly spiritual content and influence. They usually have a mystical belief in forces that transcend the material world even though they may be vague about their precise nature.

Many actors who take the teachings of the Christian religions for granted perform the extraordinary mental feat of also believing in palmistry, astrology, numerology, signs and omens. They seem to find nothing incongruous in these various loyalties which link past and present. Such an attitude is not peculiar to members of the theatrical profession of course, but it is safe to say that it is more prevalent among them than among any other special group in our population.

The actor does not habitually use practical Christianity as self-discipline in the deepest sense. His code, like that of the average man, is a synthesis of Christian doctrine, the law of the community in which he lives, and the prejudices and beliefs of the society in which he has been reared. Usually it is quite beyond the power of the ordinary person to differentiate between these three forces and it is not surprising that most actors cannot do so.

In regard to attendance at church, there is not much difference between members of the theatrical profession and that of any other section of the community. The percentage of churchgoers in relation to the total population in England has been shrinking for many years. Adults who are churchgoers tend to belong to the older age groups and this includes those who are members of the acting profession.

There is one exception to this and that is in regard to actors who are Roman Catholics. They are the most definite in their religious beliefs and usually adhere to religious observance. There are reasons why Roman Catholicism has a special appeal to the actor. Its pomp and ceremony satisfies his love of the dramatic and it was not until after the Reformation that the Church so severely penalized the actor. There had of course been difficulties between Church and stage prior to the Reformation (the fact that a Roman Catholic priest is forbidden to visit a public theatrical performance is proof enough of this) but there was little real persecution. Quite a number of converts to Roman Catholicism are actors, and many actors both in Great Britain and the United States are either Irish or Irish in origin and adhere to their traditional faith.

As far as could be gathered from answers in my questionnaire, the actor seems to be rather vague on the question of divine judgment. He seems to hope that on the day of accounting the sacred origin of his calling will win him a higher place in heaven than he might otherwise hope for.

It is not that the actor is without a sense of guilt. The attitude of the Reformed Church, of his parents and of society toward his profession ensures that he has a sense of guilt because of his decision to become an actor. Also, perhaps for this reason, he has a strong desire for atonement. The enormous energy and concentration he puts into his work is colored by this desire. It is also partly responsible for his tolerance of the failings of others and for his well-developed charitable instincts.

Most of those who make up the congregation of any Christian church are women and this is also true within the theatrical profession. Actresses are more likely to be orthodox in their religious beliefs than actors. Even those who are not regular in their church attendance usually insist that their children have a conformist religious upbringing. This does not necessarily mean that the actress is more deeply religious than the actor nor that this is true of women as a whole. Women are conformists rather than dissenters. Their nonconformity is usually the result of some deep emotional disappointment and not any philosophical discontent.

The actor who is in rebellion against religious disciplines and who finds self-discipline difficult is usually hurting only himself—his aggression turns on himself. Oddly enough, he is given no credit for his lack of aggression against individuals or systems. Because no famous actor has been in the forefront of political revolution or the leader of any movement demanding social change, he is often dismissed as frivolous and immoral. Society considers all artists to be less moral and less religious than other people are, but it is even more prejudiced against the actor.

While religious convictions may help an actor to enforce his own self-discipline, it may not always help his career if he applies strict moral judgments to the type of parts he may be called upon to play. Many great plays which are truly moral have often been regarded as immoral, and players with strong religious feelings have often felt compelled to refuse to appear in them. In other instances it may simply be that there is a part in a particular play which offends the susceptibilities of a player. For instance, in three separate productions of O'Neill's *Ah Wilderness* it was difficult to find an actress to play the role of the prostitute and impossible to get any actress to speak all the lines in this part. In each case, cuts had to be made. Usually it is actresses rather than actors who display this kind of moral squeamishness.

It is true of course that many trivial comedies are crude and vulgar, but this does not mean that they are actually immoral. However much the young actor may object to appearing in such plays, he should remember that he is only being asked to play the part and not to become the kind of person he is portraying. The time may come when only good plays are staged but it seems unlikely. In every age crude and vulgar plays have been written and produced. Sometimes plays of this kind may fail or they may be enormously successful because they provide the kind of entertainment their audiences like. Every young actor has to realize that during his career he will have all kinds of parts in all kinds of plays. He must discipline himself to accept this.

Criticism of crude and vulgar plays was expressed by many actors who replied to my questionnaire, just as it had been expressed by nearly all actors with whom I discussed this question. It may be, however, that the actor bases his criticism on moral values as well as artistic ones. If this were not so all these actors might have expressed interest in modern plays which are critical of our society. They did not do so. The actor who dreams about having his own theatre and appearing in plays of his own choice nearly always chooses the classics.

Young actors who lack self-discipline often say that this is because of the low standard of the plays in which they have to appear if they are to continue in the profession. Yet so far in Great Britain no concerted effort has been made by the profession as a whole to change the type of play usually seen in commercial theatres. Far greater efforts have been made in this direction in New York, where groups of actors have done splendid work in presenting plays of unusual caliber in various little "off Broadway" theatres.

Many critics, including the Americans and the Irish, find the English actor "genteel." There is some truth in this but it must be remembered that quite apart from social attitudes in the actor himself, the characters he is called upon to play are usually middle class or aristocratic. All critics, however, seem to admire the discipline of the English actor which enables him to wear costume as to the manner born so that the very real discomfort he often endures is never apparent.

This is the most obvious aspect of self-discipline of course, but self-discipline in the actor or actress is like the iceberg—the greater part of it is not visible to the beholder. The more delicate the task, the greater the demand on the whole personality and the powers of concentration of the person who carries it out. No work asks more of a person than the art of acting. The painter may wipe out and repaint, the writer erase and rewrite; but the impression the actor makes on each audience to whom he plays is made once and for all time. Worse still, the demand is often great when the reward is little. An actor who is given a fine part is getting back and absorbing into himself just as much as he gives. Unfortunately, for one part of this kind every actor plays—and has to play—many roles that give back little. Yet the actor who has disciplined himself may triumph in a part that would not, on first study, seem rewarding.

We may not live in an age of great contemporary plays but neither did Henry Irving or Sara Bernhardt. Both achieved enormous success in parts of a type that no modern playwright would dare to write.

CHAPTER *fourteen*

MIND AND BODY

Many people are inclined to regard the actor as a person guided by emotion rather than by intellect. This view is based on a very narrow interpretation of the word *intellect*. The dictionary defines intellect as the faculty of knowing, reasoning and understanding. What the actor has to know about is human nature, what he has to reason about is how to interpret characters, what he has to understand is the technique by which he can do this.

In learning about human nature the actor may obtain some knowledge through reading psychology or sociology but since he is concerned with individual characters and not the masses, he has to make contact with people of varied types so that he can study and observe them. If an actor has to play the part of a workingman he is not going to be able to do this by reading the works of Marx or Engels or any political philosophy, and he will only be misled and confused if he believes this to be possible.

When he has studied and observed the kind of character he is to portray, the actor then has to use his reasoning powers to transmute this knowledge into terms of acting. He has to decide not only what to put into his interpretation but what to leave out. He can only do this through a thorough knowledge of technique.

Many stage actors and an even larger number of film actors have talked to me of what they *put in* to interpreting a particular character. The trouble was that what was put in did not always *come out*. This was because they had not been able to translate the study they had put in on the character into action. All acting is expressed in action. To stand still on a stage is an act just as much as moving or speaking is an act. This is one reason why theories of acting never come from successful professional actors. A theory, in the ordinary meaning of the word, arises from speculative thought. Acting cannot be speculative. So the actor has to learn to express, through the technique of his art, what he wishes to convey to his audience.

If this were not so then there would be no need of professional actors of any kind. Everyone experiences emotions, everyone has ideas of some sort, however simple. Some film directors have taken advantage of this by taking effective shots of groups or individuals involved in dramatic situations. As a result of this, at least one director evolved a theory that here was the way to make films, and that he could dispense with professional actors altogether. He was the victim of his own theory. Retakes, when needed, were impossible, and the variety of the emotions expressed simultaneously by the different individuals in the crowd weakened or spoiled the effect the director wished to convey to the audience when the film was completed. If this director had been working in a studio with professional actors their technique would have solved his problems. The camera could have pin-pointed A who was horrified by what had happened, and gone on to B who was uninterested, and then to C who was excited. The actors could have conveyed the right emotions at the time they were required. The crowd of non-actors could only react to what was happening before their eyes, each in their own way and all at the same time.

Yet the professional actor is never merely an "instrument" of either the stage or the camera. He maintains his own distinctive character and it is through his individual abilities, his own imaginative qualities, that he will succeed.

Because the actor has to use his intellect in this very specialized way he does not always do best if he comes from a home where his father is a specialist who has to use his intellect in a more academic way. In fact a father of this type may, consciously or unconsciously, stultify the imagination of the child who has leanings toward a theatrical profession.

In my survey I made a list of the occupations of the fathers of many actors and actresses. I found they included two master bakers, a well-known chef, a musician, a music teacher, a trainer of race horses, a journalist, a jeweler, a master builder and a photographer. All were men with a good deal of intelligence and initiative so that the children grew up in an environment where skills and reasoning powers were taken for granted. It is seldom that an actor comes from a home where the father is a doctor, a scientist, a naval or military officer. The explanation for this may be that such parents are likely to have very definite and exclusive interpretations of the word *intellect* and that acting may seem to them a nonintellectual and comparatively trivial profession. This may lead to their children smothering any inclinations they may have toward acting or being unable to withstand the pressure put upon them if they make an effort to become actors. Or, if the child does persist in following his impulses to act, he may have to overcome great difficulties.

The story of an actor I shall call Leo is an example of an actor who met with great opposition in his choice of career because of his father's profession. The father was a successful lawyer who was extremely orthodox in his ideas including those he had about the profession of acting. He was a martinet and the home was in consequence a joyless place. The mother liked poetry and music in an amateurish way, possibly as an escape from the kind of life her husband had created for her. She taught her child to speak poetry and to play the piano. He became something of a prodigy. Because he was a child who found learning of any kind easy he had no very grave difficulties until he reached adolescence. He wished to become a dancer but did not have the courage to say so. Instead he entered a university and the arrangement was that he would follow in the footsteps of his father and become a lawyer. After a few years he felt he could never do this. He managed to obtain a scholarship at a school of ballet and left home. Subsequently he turned to acting instead of dancing and then won a scholarship to a drama school. His intellectual abilities and artistic flair have been of great service to him in his career as an actor but his father's attitude toward the theatrical profession had a most unfortunate effect on their relationship. It has also deprived the boy of the moral support that every struggling actor so sorely needs.

In contrast to this the story of another actor illustrates how a parent of a very different disposition and no material advantages may provide the right kind of psychological background for a young actor to develop his talent with confidence and optimism. Here is his story in his own words:

My father ran away when I was a youngster. There were three of us kids, two younger than me. My mother had to go out to work. The thing I always remember about Mother is what a character she was. She could always make us laugh, make things exciting. She did it so well we were scarcely ever sorry for ourselves. Everything was an adventure. Mother made up stories about everything. Of course we were desperately poor at times. When we had nothing Mother stole for us. There was nothing of the fashionable kleptomaniac about Mother pinching things. She did it when we were hungry or at Christmas so we could have a few things like other kids. She always managed to scrape together the money to take us to a Christmas pantomime. To me everything that happened in the pantomime was just as real as what happened at home, particularly the old scene about stealing the sausages and running away from the policeman.

If the mother had not provided her children with so much love and so much fun this young man might have turned out to be a delinquent. As it was he did not. The mother saw that her children went to school, where the boy did well. He wrote poetry that was published and through this was introduced to a theatrical manager who gave him employment. He has earned a successful living in the theatre for many years and is well adjusted to his environment. Socially he regards himself as an "outsider" rather than an "insider" and no doubt he has much in common with the mummers of a past age whose backgrounds were equally poor as far as material advantages were concerned.

Whatever his background the person who is mentally lazy, who lacks the curiosity or the ability to concentrate, cannot hope for success in the theatre. There is no easy way of overcoming the problems with which the actor has to deal, although from time to time cults spring up which purport to do this. No cult can be an effective substitute for hard study and self-education, although each cult may of course offer some enlightenment. For the intelligent actor a cult may do this even if he does nothing more than ask questions about it and analyze the answers. In this way he may help to clarify his own mind. It is a mistake to accept any cult blindly as a minority of actors do. Blind acceptance is often a form of mental laziness and cults are often created by people with oversimplified ideas. In other instances a really hard-working devotee of theatrical art may propound a theory which may be helpful, but it may be seized upon by people seeking a simple solution to difficulties of various kinds and inflated and distorted out of all proportion to its real worth. That does not mean that the original idea had no value at all.

The actor should try to keep an open mind and he must beware of labels such as "intellectual" or "anti-intellectual." To attach a label to something we do not understand does not increase our understanding. Only an impartial investigation into any new theories about acting can do that.

To reach a better understanding of this art is not only the actor's obligation but his privilege. All too often the young actor is impatient of slow progress. He sees himself as an untried race horse who starts by being entered in an unimportant race. If he wins he gets into a bigger and better race with more important horses and this process continues until he enters for the most important stakes of all. It should be remembered that a race horse is taking part in a competition in order to win. In performing a play some teamwork is necessary for success.

Whether the actor favors the idea of teamwork or not, the fact remains that only greater knowledge of all the forces that affect his art as a whole can give him genuine and lasting success. Only through increased understanding can his imagination be freed. At the present time too many young actors and actresses are floundering around in intellectual darkness so that their performances lack vitality and illumination. This darkness is not always due to mental incapacity on their part but because their capacity is not utilized. They may be handicapped by an emotional refusal to seek knowledge that may upset ready-made values and reveal vast tracts of unexplored psychological territory. Naturally they are not alone in this, as it is characteristic of human behavior as a whole. Possibly because the actor belongs to such a very ancient profession, with such strong traditions, he does not develop his faculties of *constructive* self-criticism. Where he appears to do so he is often seeking reassurance rather than enlightenment. This is a very great pity because so many theatrical values belong to the past rather than to the present.

The world is changing and society is changing more rapidly than ever before, and technical progress is far outrunning psychological understanding. The actor is the only artist who can *directly* interpret society to itself. He cannot interpret what he does not understand.

It is misleading to suggest that an actor should "lose himself" in a part. To achieve great acting he must "find" himself in a part. If he has not developed his intelligence and imagination sufficiently to understand the character he is portraying, and to understand himself in relation to it, he cannot make the audience understand the character or exactly what he is trying to do.

An actor does not need to have committed a murder in order to portray a murderer, but if he cannot imagine any circumstances in which he would feel an urge to commit murder, then he is not only deficient in imagination but ignorant of the depths of his own psychology.

Without knowledge and acceptance of what Jung calls "the dark side" of every human personality the actor is likely to act only on a superficial plane. It is from "the dark side" that many of our deepest emotions come and they may be used creatively or destructively like any other great natural force. Yet many people have such a horror of primitive emotions that they cannot bear to admit their existence in themselves. Anything that would detract from their ideals of themselves must be denied. The actor usually has a well-developed ideal of himself, so if he shuts his mind to the kind of self-realization that would help him to understand the characters he portrays he will fail.

In contrast to the pitfalls that lie in wait for the actor who does not develop his intellect and imagination along the right lines, there is that rare personality possessed of so much talent that it prevents rather than ensures complete success. Such personalities are not common but they do exist in many walks of life and are to be found in the theatre. Guy is an outstanding example of what can happen when great creative ability and imagination are allowed to run riot. Guy suffered from a surfeit of good fairies at his christening. He was, to begin with, extraordinarily good-looking. Perhaps it was because of his looks that he seemed destined for a theatrical career. Guy had nothing against this but he was equally interested in the possibility of becoming a ballet dancer, a musician, a painter or a writer. He also had an outstanding ability in learning languages. In the course of his career in the theatre he has been successful as an actor, a theatrical designer and a playwright. He has played juvenile leads in which his youthful good looks caused a sensation and he has appeared in films. He has been brilliant in revue and is now an outstanding character actor. In addition to all this he is the author of a number of books.

Naturally Guy has had a full and interesting life, but because he did not canalize his talent and energy into one medium of expression, critics have never done full justice to any of his work. He will never become the famous star actor that he might have become if he had had fewer talents.

It may be that Guy's good looks were something of a misfortune. He could scarcely have failed to have had narcissistic tendencies or to desire admiration, love and applause. He obtained these things through a dazzling display of many talents but he might have achieved the same thing through using only one of his talents, that of acting. Certainly on his appearance alone, he would have fulfilled the ideal the public has in regard to the actor.

If one puts the question "What does the typical actor look like?" to any member of the public, the reply is likely to be something like this: "Taller than average, good features and a polished manner." How far is this reply an accurate description of the typical actor? How is it that so many actors possess few of these qualities? Does not that description simply give a picture of the average playgoer's ideal of how an actor should look?

It is a sad fact that there are many unsuccessful actors with all the psychological and mental attributes needed for success who fail because of physical handicaps. One of the most usual of these is lack of height. It is true that physical appearance does not ensure success nor make failure a certainty. The actor who is below average height will point out that Kean, Garrick, and other famous stars were not tall men, but these were exceptional men and they lived in a period when theatrical conditions were very different from what they are today. Today a young English actor's first engagement is likely to be in repertory. A repertory manager prefers to engage an actor of medium height because he can play a greater variety of roles. The undersized actor is not likely to be cast for heroic or romantic roles, and if he is, he is not likely to establish himself as a favorite in such roles. So he may have to struggle along, biding his time until he has passed his first youth and his lack of height is not prejudicial to his playing the many character parts available to the older man.

The too tall player also has troubles. The late Sir Aubrey Smith had far greater success in middle and old age than he ever had as a young actor. Established male stars do not care to play opposite a youngster who towers over them. Leading ladies do not want a leading man who dwarfs them.

Whatever talent the too short or unusually tall actor may have, he causes endless difficulties to the director in the stage grouping. I have seen plays in which there had to be a perpetual "cheating" to get over the difficulties created by a male star who is too short and of a female star who is taller than average. One had to sit or lie while the other stood, and the tall leading lady was compelled to wear sandals with flat heels.

A friend of mine trained as an actor and then had to content himself with backstage work because he was six foot four.

It must be accepted that when anything unusual in the physical appearance is going to present the stage director with a problem, the actor concerned has a tremendous handicap.

All this may seem too obvious to be worth mentioning. Yet everyone who has anything to do with training drama students is aware that aspirants are never deterred by their own physical limitations. The explanation is that reason does not dictate the actor's choice of career.

Naturally, physical appearance does not ensure success or make failure a certainty. Yet the short actor is always haunted by his handicap. He has probably been acutely conscious of it from an early age. He may bolster up his ego by pointing out that little men are more aggressive than larger ones. They have to be. In all walks of life, including the theatre, there are undersized men who have made good. But when such men have succeeded in the theatre they have had very great talent. One of the most beautiful faces ever to appear in the British *Spotlight* was that of an actor with the physique of a fourteen-year-old. He received many calls but few engagements and had to leave the theatre. Once the undersized actor is in a position to choose his own parts he may enjoy success, but it becomes more and more difficult for him to make a beginning. Both stage and film directors are likely to pass him over for a player of average height.

Another characteristic of the undersized man is that he longs to shine above his fellows so that he may compensate himself for the humiliations he has suffered. It may be this aggressiveness that drives him to a stage career rather than any humble desire to serve a great art.

On the other hand, one sphere is favorable to him if he is psychologically suited to it. It is as true historically as today that most great comedians and comedy actors have been small men. They have, however, usually had enough insight to accept their physical appearance and to use their talent to exploit themselves for what they are and not for what they would like to be. Charles Chaplin, one of the greatest of them, has gone farther. Again and again he has made fun of the small man—the David who aspires to play Goliath. He has made fun of the world which judges a man by his inches. But Chaplin did not succeed because he was a short man determined not to let his shortness handicap him. He owes his success to his own genius as an artist. There are great actors irrespective of size, just as there are bad or mediocre actors of all sizes.

It may be asked why, if comedy roles favor the undersized actor, he does not naturally turn to comedy from the beginning. The answer is to be found in the curious attitude taken toward the art of comedy. Not only is the small man anxious to compensate for his handicap by playing roles on the stage that he could not play in real life, but comedy is regarded as second best. That the clown longs to play Hamlet is a cliché but nonetheless true. The adolescent who has emotional drives toward acting never even considers comedy. The psychology of the adolescent who does turn toward comedy in the first place is such that he is attracted toward the music hall, musical comedy or films. I have never yet met one youngster coming for stage training in a drama school who had the ambition to be a great comedian. I can recall two actors below medium height whom I advised, right from the beginning, to concentrate on comedy, but neither of them would take this advice. They regarded it as some sort of slight. It took one of them six years to come round to my point of view. He is quite brilliant in comedy roles now. The other took a great many more years to realize that he was best suited to comedy and he also was quite outstanding in the first comedy part he played. Comedy acting is a supreme art, different from dramatic acting, and the two arts are not comparable. It is ironic that while critics take the view that comedy acting is inferior to dramatic acting, when great comedians do emerge the critics build up a mystique around their art, as happened with Chaplin, the Marx Brothers and Danny Kaye.

Whatever an actor's physical appearance may be, good health is extremely important. It may be asked, "What is good health? Does not success and a contented existence make for good health?" It is certainly true that failure and discontent may cause bad health but it is also true that nobody whose general physical condition is poor or whose nervous system is unstable can hope to get through those early difficult years on the stage unscathed or to sustain success once it is gained. One of the finest English actors of the past twenty years had his career wrecked by ill-health and died at a relatively early age; another, of unusual talent and personality, collapsed just when fame was on his doorstep.

Drama schools now quite rightly discourage students lacking stamina. Unfortunately many of those who have found a delicate constitution a handicap in real life are, like the undersized man, driven toward stage careers by the wish to enact roles they could never sustain in actuality.

CHAPTER *fifteen*

THE PSYCHOLOGY OF
SUCCESS

Nearly all young actors and actresses are keenly aware of the impressions they make on other people whether they are preoccupied with other people's reactions or not. They also seem to have more definite pictures of themselves than the non-actor has, but these pictures are prejudiced and are affected by moods. The personal portrait presented by many of those who replied to my questionnaire was not the same as the analysis of their answers to questions revealed. It was significant that the less insight the individuals had into their own characters and motivations, the less success they enjoyed. In some instances they were debilitated by self-pity, or thought they were unsuccessful because of an altruistic nobility of character which prevented them from using stratagems that were freely used by less scrupulous competitors to obtain employment. Or else they were defeated by fellow actors who were far more aggressive in their attempts to obtain employment.

It must be remembered, however, that when a large part of anyone's force or energy is devoted to the conquest of material things he is on far less dangerous ground than he who wishes to make a conquest over people. A young businessman gains success through his commercial instincts and abilities. The embryo actor has his origin in the child who wants to conquer hearts and for him success is much more difficult to attain.

Conflicting as the character of each actor may be and complex as all the circumstances that influence him are, a shadowy picture of the typical successful actor did emerge from my survey.

His position in the family does not seem to be very important. This is probably due to the fact that a child, whether he is the eldest, the youngest or one of any number, may have various reasons for wishing to win hearts. The economic situation in the actor's home does influence his future of course. The parents of a small family are likely to be able to provide their children with better accommodation, better food and a better education than the parents of a large family are able to do. These things give the child an advantage, so the successful actor is more likely to have come from a small family rather than a large one. Also he is likely to have had a mother or a satisfactory mother substitute who gave him loving care. As a child he has enjoyed greater privileges than he could hope for in the outside world. The actor who finds success usually feels a great gratitude toward his mother and shares the rewards of his success with her.

The father of a successful actor is likely to have had far less influence over him. Sometimes the father may have died at an early age or have been away from home a great deal. Whatever the reason, the influence of the father has usually been weaker than that of the mother or has been rejected altogether.

In childhood some successful actors have been less robust than their more athletic companions, although they have seldom been the victims of real delicacy or ill-health.

Many actors have not enjoyed their childhood wholeheartedly but it seems doubtful if any really imaginative children do. Some successful actors have been unhappy children but most of them look back on their childhood as a mixture of happiness and unhappiness.

Often they have been good all-round scholars at school or at least have excelled in certain subjects such as English literature. They have usually found games boring and school life boring as a whole.

The successful actor is, and thinks of himself as, a sensitive fellow but he is not always sure if other people think the same. To gain success he may hurt other people's feelings but does not always know that he has done so. He looks upon hard knocks, given and taken, as part of the hazards of success. He is likely to value courage as being the finest human quality. It might be imagined that this conviction would be shared by actors of all types, successful or otherwise. According to the results of my questionnaire this was not so. I also made a point of asking this question of actors as well as many people in other walks of life. I found that all those who put courage first were people who were either successful already or seemed likely to achieve success. In the questionnaire, actors who were not successful or who seemed unlikely to make great progress never put courage as the finest human quality. The qualities that were high on their list seemed to suggest that they might have regarded courage as one of the more Philistine virtues.

The successful actor feels that he must spend some time alone for study and recuperation but he dislikes solitude and prefers to be with others. It might be supposed that all actors would express this opinion but many did not.

The successful actor feels that his talent and intelligence are above the average. It may be argued that all actors think this and would not aspire to be actors if they did not. What is certain, however, is that the actor who did not think so would scarcely have the staying power to achieve success in the face of serious setbacks or obstacles.

The successful actor does not think very much about his personal appearance except when it affects his work. Great actors are seldom dandies and some of the most famous are usually careless in their dress.

The successful actor does not worry about the opinions of others unless they have an influence on his professional standing. As a contrast I have observed that many unsuccessful actors are unduly sensitive to the opinions of others.

One question asked in the questionnaire was: "What person, living or dead, do you most admire?" It was significant that a number who were reasonably successful mentioned their mothers as the most admirable character they had ever known. Many people in other walks of life have a particular idol, a person who may be living or dead but notable in some way. It may be that if the successful actor had a niche reserved for an idol, he himself occupies it. If his mother occupies the niche it is because of what she has given to him and not because of anything she may have given to the world as a whole.

The majority of actors like an active life full of changes and stimulations that enlarge the imagination. Some of the unsuccessful ones who answered the questionnaire expressed a desire for a more settled existence but the successful ones either disliked the idea of settling down or expressed the view that they put their work first and thought little about their domestic background.

In reply to a question about reading and choice of books in childhood it seemed clear that as far as the successful were concerned it was visits to the theatre that had made an indelible impression rather than any particular book read at an early age.

No actor is very much concerned with material wealth but the successful actor is less concerned with it than the less successful. He does not dream of wealth which would enable him to have his own theatre where he could shine because he has sufficient confidence in himself to feel that managements will be quite willing to offer him the parts he desires to play.

The successful actor is not concerned with "schools" or methods of acting. He has worked out his own method and intends to stick to it.

I have heard the view expressed by some disgruntled actors, chafing against their own limitations, that the successful actor of today owes his success and his confidence to the fact that he has come from a wealthy background. This is not the case, because the child of wealthy parents is seldom called upon to exercise his imagination in order to get what he wants. The background typical of the successful modern actor is one in which difficulties in following his bent did exist but could be overcome.

However favorable his background, the would-be actor has some difficulties or handicaps to overcome before he can achieve success. What the beginner has to strive for is self-understanding. He needs self-understanding before he can decide whether or not the struggle ahead will be worth the effort he will have to put into it. He also has to ask himself whether success, if it comes, will compensate him for what he has to undertake and what he has to give up during the long hard journey.

In the beginning all young actors feel that nothing in life is worth while unless they can become actors. The successful actor has to continue to hold that view throughout his entire career. He has to hold it in spite of the fact that he laughs ruefully over his stage-struck youth when he believed that he would soon have "a break" that would make continual success a certainty.

It may be that if young actors were not stage-struck and did not have the illusion that one "break" was going to solve all their problems, they might weaken in their early struggles more easily than they do. With first success new horizons open up, but each advance brings its own difficulties. The successful actor is one who, at each phase of his career, faces the difficulties inherent in the position he has reached.

The actor who is most fortunate is the one to whom success comes slowly enough for him to consolidate each advance. In this way he can overcome the enemies of success, which may be in his own psychic make-up, as he goes along. He can also develop increased knowledge and technique of his own craft as he advances. The actor who makes an overnight success a few years after he leaves drama school is at a tremendous disadvantage since he is competing with veterans.

The actor who is boosted swiftly to film stardom is in an even more perilous position than the stage actor. Usually he has had too little dramatic training and little acting experience. He is too young to have matured in any way and is confronted with many psychological dangers.

"I have never had any lessons in dramatic training," one young star told me with complacent pride. The inference was, of course, that she had so much natural ability that training was superfluous. After a couple of years her film contract was ended and was never renewed. Many beginners would learn a salutary lesson if they could study the casts—including the stars—of films covering the period when the war ended to the present day. So many young actors and actresses were boosted to stardom, so few have survived as stars. Once a player has reached the top there is nowhere to go except down. A few intrepid characters do scale the heights again on their own merits, but to the majority success comes but once and never returns.

It must be conceded that it takes great strength of character to reject an easy opportunity for success if such an opportunity comes. Quite apart from the delights of the more obvious aspects of success, there is another point to be considered. Almost all intelligent members of the theatrical profession are aware that there are many quite successful actors with star quality whom managements never seem to star. So the youngster offered an opportunity which it might be wisest to ignore says to himself, "Look at So-and-So, he's one of the most terrific actors I've ever seen and has been for ten years but he is still playing second fiddle." This is a fact and one which is not due to any personal or psychological handicaps in the actors concerned. The fact that this situation exists is an additional spur to the youngster offered a star part too soon to accept with alacrity. However, the fact remains that nearly all our truly great and well-established stars of today did have struggles as young actors. They not only had struggles to develop their talent to the full but they knew the frustration of playing poor parts, of being miscast and even of proving inadequate in parts they had longed to play. A study of their careers is confirmation, if any were needed, that the successful actor owes his success not only to his talent but to his courage, persistence and powers of endurance. An actor's success must come, in part, from faith in himself. It is easy to travel hopefully, it is more difficult to travel when hope has gone and only faith remains, faith that one has something worth giving to the world.

This faith must be based on truth and reality otherwise it is not really faith, it is fantasy, the kind of fantasy that has led many an actor to tragedy.

CHAPTER sixteen

BOOTH THE ASSASSIN

The story of John Wilkes Booth is that of an actor who never could bring himself to give up fantasies when faced by reality. He was a neurotic who brought a nation to the verge of disaster. The assassination of Abraham Lincoln had deep, pervasive and lasting results which have influenced political feelings in the United States right down to the present time.

John Wilkes Booth's crime may be dismissed as that of a madman but this explains nothing. At the time of Lincoln's assassination mentally ill people probably formed much the same proportion of the total population as they do today, with, in Great Britain and in the United States, one in every eight hospital beds occupied by a psychically ill person. Since the science of psychiatry was not developed until the last years of the nineteenth century, little was done about such people unless they broke the law or became public nuisances. Until he assassinated Lincoln, the youngest of the Booth brothers had neither broken the law nor made himself a public nuisance.

When the psychotic commits his first act of violence it is almost always an explosion resulting from pressure of external events reacting on internal conflict. Reality becomes unbearable and the victim seeks relief in violence against himself or others. In 1865, heritage, environment and the climate of the time combined to produce a flash point in John Wilkes Booth.

The Booth brothers came of theatrical stock. Junius Brutus Booth, born in 1796 into a cultured middle-class family, was, as a youth, of a romantic and somewhat reckless temperament. He pained his family by refusing to follow the profession of his father who was a lawyer and announced that he wished to become an actor. His looks and temperament were in his favor and even at seventeen he was already known as a young man about town. With these advantages he succeeded in obtaining a small part before the end of his seventeenth year.

Success came early at that particular time. It was only a few years previously that the thirteen-year-old child prodigy, William Betty, had played leading Shakespearean roles at London's Covent Garden Theatre, supported by a galaxy of adult stars. So it was not remarkable that by the time young Booth was twenty he had already played leading roles. Indeed, his Richard III was favorably compared with that of Kean.

The young actor then played with Kean in Drury Lane. The two appear to have had much in common.

Violent behavior and intemperance were a fashion of the time. Nevertheless there were limits beyond which an actor could not go if he was to keep his hold on popular affection—as Kean was to find to his cost later on. Booth, who had already married, soon became bored with his young wife and conceived a violent infatuation for a Bow Street flower seller whom he flaunted in the face of the public. Angered by the criticism that resulted, the young actor decided to go to the United States, taking the girl with him. It is probable that professional jealousy also influenced this decision. The Booths were ever impatient for fame. Junius had had to play second fiddle to Kean for several seasons and he could see no hope of supplanting the older actor. This may have been an additional reason for flight.

Booth made his American debut in Richmond, Virginia, in 1821 when he was twenty-five. Later the actor and his love, whose name was Mary Ann, moved to Belair, Maryland.

There was no easy divorce in those days. It was thirty years later, and only one year before his death, that Booth's wife divorced him and he was able to marry Mary Ann. The pair had never had anything in common but sexual attraction and the first fine frenzy had not long survived the sordid realities of their situation and the uncertainties of theatrical life.

During the years 1821 to 1839 Mary Ann brought ten children into the world. Her husband, always poorly adjusted, had by that time degenerated into an intemperate melancholic.

A number of the children, perhaps fortunately for all concerned, died young. Three of the boys survived and became actors; the eldest was Junius Brutus junior, the second surviving son was Edwin and the youngest was John Wilkes. He was born when Junius was eighteen and Edwin was six. Their respective ages are important in view of what happened later on.

John was only a little over thirteen when his father died on a Mississippi steamboat. Edwin, who had been touring with his father for about three years, stepped into his shoes—he took over and played the part of Richard III when he was only nineteen.

It is to be doubted if the younger members of the family felt much grief at their father's death. He had been a difficult, moody man and in any event they had seen little of him because, after an initial appearance in New York, he spent most of his years touring. He is said to have excelled in tragic parts and but for his temperament might have had considerable success. As it was, the family never knew anything but financial and emotional crises and periods of real poverty and deprivation.

It was the youngest children who suffered most from their father's instability. John, a handsome child with well-cut features, flashing eyes and a slender figure, had a passionate desire to follow in the footsteps of his two brothers and become an actor. Longing for greatness, he brooded and fretted and was consumed by impatience. Had not William Betty been a star at Covent Garden by the time he was thirteen? John chafed at inaction and rebelled against the decision of his father, his eldest brother and Edwin that he should not start his career at an early age. To John, his father and eldest brother—who had been a man when John was born—seemed united against him. He longed to prove himself. John felt even more bitter toward Edwin. He could remember playing childish games with Edwin and yet Edwin had left home to join their father's company three years previously. Now he was a leading actor. John was consumed by a burning envy and jealousy of his brother.

All the Booths reveled in Shakespearean roles. This was the fashion of the time. They specialized in such parts as Othello, Macbeth and Richard III. To the small boy John such parts and their players must have merged into an overpowering symbol of oppression.

The life of the family still seemed to revolve around the trio even when they were absent. His resentment and frustration mounting, John became more and more difficult. His tantrums sometimes terrified his adoring sisters, who had always petted and cosseted this youngest member of the family. Edwin, like Junius, had seemed to pass all too swiftly from childhood to manhood, they were too powerful and remote to inspire protective love. John was different. He was a charmer when he wanted to be, his smile could be irresistible and his gaiety infectious; but his rages and despair could be terrifying. The sisters begged him to be patient; they could do little else.

Ten weary years passed before Edwin gave John the chance for which he had waited. At the age of twenty-eight, after almost a decade of increasing success, Edwin took over the Winter Garden Theatre in New York. Junius, never a star of first magnitude but with a sound reputation as an actor and manager, joined him in the venture. They staged a magnificent season of Shakespeare, and Junius, Edwin and John played together in *Julius Caesar*. Played together in a tragedy about the assassination of a ruler of a great state, whom his assassins regarded as a tyrant.

John, who had only scored provincial successes without the help of his brothers, now had the opportunity to outshine them.

How did John feel as he stood in the wings waiting to go on? Here was the culmination of all the long years of dreaming, planning and struggling. The opportunity had come to prove that he was a great actor—to prove it to himself, to prove it to the public, to prove it to that loved, hated and envied brother Edwin, who was the adored idol of the American public. Was the strain too much? Did the ambivalence of his feelings make John's performance less good than it might have been? Edwin Booth was not a subtle man. If he had had greater insight perhaps he would never have subjected his oversensitive young brother to the ordeal of that night. He had reached a peak in his own career, he could afford to be generous and give his brother a good part, but it is unlikely that he ever regarded John's New York debut as a threat to his own unique position.

The first night was a tremendous success but no one acclaimed the performance of the youngest Booth as finer than that of Edwin. More than ever John felt victimized. Was he not the best-looking, the most charming of the brothers, had he not greater fire and subtlety than Edwin? He knew women adored him. His sisters might have been the first to succumb to his charm but they were not the last. John never succeeded in outshining Edwin but he did succeed in becoming a matinee idol, a pin-up boy of his time whose presence in a theatre brought women clustering around the stage door. He was a King of Hearts but not a monarch in the world of great dramatic acting.

How much truth was there in John's conviction that he could be as great an actor as Edwin? Opinion seems to have been divided. Some averred that John might have become a great actor, others that he was an eccentric exhibitionist with small talent. It is possible that he did have talent but that it was deflected and weakened by his overwhelming anxiety to triumph over Edwin. Impartial assessment of his work was impossible after the cataclysm; before it he was not sufficiently well known for serious critics to have given judgment.

The season at the Winter Garden had been a success but meanwhile a greater drama was moving onto a larger stage. The Civil War had begun.

As with all wars, it served as a focal point for the conflicts of the emotionally disturbed. As defeat moved over the Southern States, John Wilkes Booth became a more and more fervid supporter of a lost cause. At first his patriotic outpourings had been taken as yet another pose of one who had become a notorious poseur. His fanaticism verged on the absurd even in a society in which high temper and aristocratic contempt for the plebian Northerners was customary.

Opinion is divided as to whether Booth assassinated Lincoln because jealousy of Edwin unhinged his mind or because he believed he was striking a blow for the Southern cause. It seems more likely that in the mind of John Wilkes two lost causes had become one. He, the unappreciated genius, should have been able to triumph over his family; and the armies of the Southern States should have been able to triumph over their uncultured Northern brothers. In killing the father of the American people, Lincoln's assassin was also killing his own father and the elder brothers who had become father surrogates standing between him and the realization of his dreams of fame.

It was only three years after the performance of *Julius Caesar* at the Winter Garden Theatre that the assassination took place. In the meanwhile Edwin had gone from triumph to triumph in that same theatre. Only a year before his young brother murdered Lincoln, Edwin had broken a theatrical record. He had played Hamlet for one hundred consecutive performances. In hearing Edwin's performance lauded to the skies John Wilkes must have drained the cup of bitterness to the dregs. No actor likes to hear another actor praised. If the play had not been *Hamlet* the younger brother might not have suffered such anguish. Of all the Booth men, father and brothers, was not he, John, the most obvious choice for Hamlet? He had wanted to play the part for years. He felt he had an uncanny understanding of the character. In fact he *was* Hamlet. Had not a usurper, aided by two others, robbed him of his rightful heritage? For him, the three were a hated entity. His father, like the King in *Hamlet,* had ruled a small kingdom and would not give it up. Also, because of his actions, his children were illegitimate. This had deprived them of the sort of social life to which they were entitled. Was not Junius, the elder brother, counseling wisdom and patience, like Polonius but a much stronger and more powerful figure than Shakespeare's old rat behind the arras? And Edwin, was he not the most hateful of the three rivals?

Jealousy is an emotion which is depised by society and no individual cares to admit, even to himself, that he is guilty of feeling it. So jealousy had to be disguised and in his conscious mind the jealous person usually sees himself as a victim of injustice. John could not kill his father even if he had ever consciously desired to do so, because his father was already dead. It was only in the minds of his audiences that he still lived, admired as an actor despite his failings. It was the achievements of the father and the far greater achievements of Junius junior, and of Edwin in particular, which John wished to destroy. He had tried to do this by proving himself a greater actor than any of them but had been denied a fair chance because Edwin had never given him leading roles. So for months he brooded over the problem of finding some way in which he could prove his own greatness. It had to be some act which would make him famous in the eyes of the whole world so that the achievements of his father and brothers would seem pitiful by comparison.

Up to this time John Wilkes had never had any serious interest in politics. He was not associated with any political organization. Now he tried to become an associate of the political leaders in the Southern States. They refused to take him seriously and he talked so wildly that they soon fought shy of him. They were practical men faced with practical problems and Booth had no constructive ideas. Although he did not openly voice any suggestions that Lincoln should be assassinated, his whole attitude filled them with disgust and they considered him irresponsible if not unbalanced. Rejected and resentful, Booth proceeded to seek a few men who would follow where he would lead. A deadly blow must be delivered against the hated North. He had great difficulty in finding any followers, which is scarcely remarkable. From the historical material available it is not clear whether Booth had consciously planned the assassination of President Lincoln first and then conceived the idea of obtaining a political following in order to carry it out. It seems more likely that to begin with he may have seen himself as a male Joan of Arc who was going to arouse and lead the defeated South to victory, and when this was impossible, he changed his plans so that he could accomplish the feat and almost unaided.

There were many reasons why the plan to kill Lincoln should have a deep emotional appeal to a man of Booth's character. To begin with, the hated North had as its figurehead, as the father of its people, a man named Abraham, a man called after the most unbending of the Patriarchs, a man with a monumental head, stern prophetic eyes, jutting brow, formidable nose. He even had the beard which is the eternal symbol of the mythical, all-powerful father figure.

If the President had had another name, if he had been a small plump man and clean shaven, it is possible that Booth might never have seen him as the symbol of all he hated. Lincoln might have sat through the performance at Ford's Theatre on that fateful night and walked out unharmed.

The killing of the President did not do anything to help the cause of the Southern States and could not have done so in any case. Killing the father of the American people did give Booth the emotional catharsis he had to have. By that one act he had revenged himself on both the living and the dead. Symbolically he had "killed" the North, the enemy, and in doing so he became the most talked-of man in the Western world.

Whether up to the time of the assassination Booth really expected to be acclaimed a national hero is not known. He had planned nothing but his escape after the killing and does not seem to have thought beyond it.

Even his revenge was not as complete as he had hoped. His brothers did suffer and Edwin became gloomy and morose for the rest of his life. Perhaps he was haunted by a guilty feeling that he was partly responsible for what his brother had done. His career was not destroyed. The nation, after recovering from its shock, turned again to its favorite actor. This is an extraordinary indication of the hold Edwin must have had over his audiences. Junius was also able to regain his place in the theatre. Both brothers lived to old age and Edwin's statue stands in Gramercy Park, New York City.

When the name Booth is mentioned in Great Britain it is usually known only to theatrical people who associate it with Edwin, who visited London and acted with Henry Irving. Only the psychologist finds the tragic young John the most interesting of the Booth brothers. Yet actors might find him interesting. John Wilkes Booth *was* a victim, the victim of his own personality. It was the furies of jealousy that drove the actor to fire the shot that shook the Western world.

CHAPTER seventeen

TWO ACTRESSES

Nothing, it would seem, is more important to the success of the stage player than to be born in the right place at the right time. In fact all the great romantic figures of history are those who seemed to be an archetype of their period. If this had not been so, many notorious or famous personalities, from Beau Brummel to Napoleon, might have remained in obscurity.

No three actresses could have been more different in appearance, character and personality than were Rachel, Eleonora Duse and Ellen Terry. Yet each represented a female type which embodied a popular ideal of their time and environment: Rachel, the type of imperious beauty much admired by the French of the mid-nineteenth century; Eleonora, the tragic heroine, sacrificing all for love in the best operatic tradition; Ellen Terry, the child-woman, a type which has always had a special appeal to British—and American—people. Mary Pickford was also in this tradition.

Rachel, Duse and Ellen Terry triumphed professionally despite the damage they inflicted on their own careers by indulging their impetuous passions.

Not only were they enormously successful on stage but they influenced their contemporaries in the way that certain film players do today. Each had her imitators, each was an inspiration to playwrights of her time. Where would Scribe have been without Rachel? If there had been no Duse, would D'Annunzio ever have been known as a playwright? Barrie and Shaw both owe a debt to Ellen Terry because, although she was too old to play their youthful heroines, she was certainly the inspiration for them. From *Alice Sit by the Fire* to *What Every Woman Knows* one can see the imprint of the Terry personality on the mind of the author.

It has been said that the whimsical, impulsive and capricious heroines of Shaw are impossible women. Yet when Shaw wrote the part of Lady Cecily Waynflete in *Captain Brassbound's Conversion* for Ellen Terry, the play enjoyed a success which it has never since achieved.

Of this trio of great romantics, Rachel, whose real name was Élisa Félix, was the first to be born. She came into the world in 1820, daughter of a poor Jewish family. Driven by necessity, the family made a long and painful migration to Paris while she was still a small child. They encountered great hardships, but like many of their kind were driven onward by the feeling that however bad their future might be it could be no worse than their past.

Papa Félix was a character of many conflicts and the family danced to his tune. He was tenacious yet unpredictable, violent but sentimental, and while ruthless and unscrupulous, was hypersensitive about anything he considered an aspersion on his honor.

Soon after they arrived in Paris, Élisa and her sister

crept out to sing in the streets, lightheaded with hunger. When their escapade became known, no impoverished aristocrat could have put on a more grandly tragic scene than their haughty father. Nevertheless the two children were allowed to continue with their pitiful efforts to earn money.

The elder sister later obtained an engagement on the lighter stage but Papa Félix soon conceived the notion that by making Élisa a great dramatic actress he could put money in his purse and at the same time satisfy his inflated sense of honor. He announced that he would himself instruct his daughter, although his qualifications for the task were shadowy. What he did have was a demonic passion for work—when he could bully others into doing it. Élisa's elder cousin, Julie Bernat, was pressed into sharing the studies. She was an enterprising young woman well able to take care of herself. She soon broke away to carve her own earnings. For years Papa Félix was to accuse her of the basest ingratitude. This made him all the more determined that Élisa, the only investment he had ever made which looked like being a success, was going to meet what he considered to be her obligations.

After a while Élisa attracted the notice of someone who introduced her to an actor named Saint-Aulaire and she studied under him at the old Théâtre Molière. She was playing parts at the age of thirteen. Even then it seems that she may have begun to develop the possessiveness that she was to display later in life toward objects of her affection. Saint-Aulaire did not seem too happy about the situation although he did believe the girl had potential talent. He suggested that she was tending to become a puppet of his teaching and that it would be better if she went to a real drama school. When these suggestions came to the ears of Papa Félix the repercussions were shattering. Papa had expected a lightning initiation into the art of great acting which would make Élisa rich in the shortest time possible. Could not his daughter accomplish miracles? Élisa herself agreed with Saint-Aulaire, gritting her teeth to hang on stubbornly during the dreadful scenes at home. She did go to the Conservatoire. She was barely sixteen when the pressure Papa brought to bear on his highly strung daughter—and on everyone else even remotely concerned with her affairs—resulted in the girl leaving the Conservatoire to take acting engagements. By the time she was seventeen she was already a well-known actress at the Gymnase Théâtre.

The records of Élisa's childhood and adolescence read like the feverish imaginings in a novel by George Sand. The Félix family was always one step ahead of destitution, and Papa could be depended upon to raise emotional storms of the first magnitude. There were outbursts about his humiliating poverty, the ingratitude of his daughters, and the jealousy which inspired others to upset his plans. He predicted the dreadful fate of the family if Élisa was not a success, the dizzy triumphs if only she would obey Papa's edicts implicitly.

It was inevitable that the girl should develop hair-trigger reactions, suffer an almost psychopathic sense of insecurity together with a touch of the persecution mania so often found in the Jewish refugee from stormy Central Europe. Also and perhaps most dynamic was the egotism which is often the product of such a background.

As a further spur to his daughter, Papa harped on the great past of the Jewish race in general and of the Félix family in particular. He was vague about the details in regard to the Félix family. It may be that their fame existed only in Papa's fervid imagination. However, his influence was not without effect. The letters and diaries of

Rachel show that in her private fantasies she had become a symbol of womanhood, triumphant and irresistible. Was it not true, she asked herself as a young girl, that her master was cold to her because his wife was jealous of the power of this pet pupil?

She had no doubt of this power. Had she not charmed Jules Janin, the formidable critic and misanthrope, into singing her praises? It was said that Janin only did this for a young actress in return for certain favors. There were rumors about the extent to which Rachel had granted favors to this notorious satyr—many people who had regarded the girl as a beautiful, talented and pathetic young thing now began to see her in a different light.

Rachel passed on to new conquests. Samson, the famous actor, the Sun God of Rachel's imaginings, now tutored the still immature young actress. In return Rachel adored him extravagantly just as she had adored Saint-Aulaire. A shade of coolness in his manner would cast her into the depths of despair. She felt sure someone was trying to turn him against her. Praise from him raised her to heaven. Throughout her life all Rachel's emotional experiences were to move from elation to depression at the speed of an express elevator. This feverish emotionalism affected her health and stamina and she alternated between frenzied activity and exhaustion.

Nevertheless her demon drove her on. Her next part was always the crucial one. Then the first night. Was she really good? What had Janin written? What did Saint-Aulaire think? Did Samson truly believe she was great? He had said so of course, yet she was not sure of the meaning of that expression in his eye, that ghost of an inflection in his voice. These fears kept her awake night after night.

Her appetite for love and approval was insatiable and when she had them she questioned their value.

Nothing could remove the sense of insecurity of the destitute refugee child hidden in the soul of Rachel. Her love affairs became notorious. She was not satisfied until each man within her orbit became her slave, and when he did she soon began to doubt his worth and to go on to fresh conquests. She had noble lovers and wealthy lovers, men who could heap wealth and fame on her and offer her social distinction through her association with them. This glamorous notoriety and her electrifying performances combined to make her a public idol of her day. She was her own best press agent. Her costumes, her carriages and her fads were a never-ending source of entertainment to the public. What had Rachel done now? Who was her latest conquest?

Yet nothing could satisfy Rachel's lust for more resounding success and ever-increasing adoration. Like her father she was touchy. Was not the lover of the moment too possessive? Was she not the one to grant favors? Always she sought to preserve her independence once she had broken free of her father. She spent her own earnings with the same prodigality with which she squandered the money of her lovers.

While wasting so much of her energy in the drama of her personal life she was, at the same time, obsessed with the desire to play some particular part in such a way that it would give her a secure place among the immortals of the theatre. Her tremendous successes ranged from the classics to the latest confection of Scribe. She had the ability possessed by so many great actresses to make a good part seem magnificent and a poor one seem good.

It was impossible that her physique could survive the stresses she imposed on it. The overwork, the emotional storms, the ecstasies and the quarrels took their inevitable toll. Rachel became a legend in her lifetime partly, one suspects, because she succumbed to tuberculosis while at the height of her powers, when she was thirty-eight. She remained a legend not only because of her achievements as an actress but also because those who found her personality intolerable were able to feel the greatest admiration for her once she had ceased to plague them.

In 1859, a year after Rachel died, Eleonora Duse was born. Her family was also poor and rootless. They were strolling players and had been for several generations. Not for them a wild dream that a daughter would become an internationally famous star and make their fortunes. They had the cynical stoicism of the unsuccessful professional. They were concerned only with what lay immediately ahead, where their next engagement would be, where their next meal was coming from and where they would sleep that night.

Eleonora began to play child parts at the age of four when she was already inured to chronic undernourishment, occasional acute hunger, cold, dirt and all the miseries of the poverty-stricken itinerant.

She was humble and fearful, like a traveler in a dark and threatening forest, and was ever to remain so. Like Rachel, however, she had her dreams. These were not dreams of conquest and triumph over all hearts but of encountering some mighty and benevolent force that would lift her out of the sordid realities of her existence. She was from childhood a mystic with a great desire to find a god on earth. If she had not met D'Annunzio she would probably have invested someone else with the qualities she worshiped and her fate would have been the same. Her innate masochism destined Eleonora for tragedy both in real life and in the parts she played.

Unlike Rachel, she was a shy adolescent who did not seek to attract men but shrank from them. She lived in an inner world of her own and, perhaps because she had been born in the theatre, accepted her future as an actress without question. Theatrical life as she knew it could scarcely have inspired her dreams.

Eleonora, after some small success in her father's Company, was frightened rather than elated at the offer of an engagement by another management. However, she was persuaded that she really might make some success and, with much misgiving, left the protection of her family.

It was the misfortune of this dark, slender girl with the haunted eyes that she aroused protective instincts only in those who could not help her much. She attracted men at first glance but her remoteness, her preoccupation with some world they could not enter, deflected their interest. Various people who had a disinterested affection for her and admired her talent and beauty did try to help. Yet Duse remained apart and alone. The deprivations which she had suffered in childhood, material and social, left an indelible mark. A sense of inadequacy was always with her, but she was indifferent to her own best interests and incapable of handling her own affairs successfully.

Yet fame came to her. Perhaps it came because of what she was rather than through what she did. In action on the stage she seems to have been the victim rather than the distiller of her own emotions. Excessively nervous and overwrought, it was when Duse stood motionless that she made the deepest impression on audiences and critics. She came to London in 1895 when Shaw was at the beginning of his theatrical career and working as a critic. He acclaimed her as being the greatest actress in the world. One of Duse's personal quirks was that she refused to wear theatrical make-up. This marred her characterizations in later years but when Shaw saw her she was still young and beautiful. Shaw was entranced because he saw her blush in a certain scene. Several times in later years he inserted a stage direction in his scripts telling the actor to blush.

Success brought Duse neither the happiness nor the security she longed for. She remained remote, playing on the stage of her inner consciousness some drama known only to herself. Then came the event that was at once the greatest climax and the point of no return in her life. She met an Italian poet called Rapagnetta, later to be known as Count Gabriele D'Annunzio.

Duse's name and career are now so closely linked with the plays and life of D'Annunzio that it is almost forgotten that she was thirty years old and a successful actress when she met him. She had become famous not through playing in literary or poetic dramas but in popular successes such as *The Lady of the Camellias, Tosca* and *Feodora*. It was D'Annunzio, the megalomaniac autocrat, who persuaded his infatuated adorer that the kind of play he wrote was the pinnacle of dramatic art.

All her life Duse had pined for a man she could believe to be truly great, and now, to her own undoing, she met him. She saw her lover not only as the greatest man of his own time but of any time—an opinion with which D'Annunzio agreed. At first he was delighted that the most famous actress in Italy shared his own convictions. She could be so immensely useful to him. Later, when she could neither persuade managements to continue putting on his plays for her nor raise more money to do so herself, he became bored.

In the first glorious morning of their association, however, he succeeded in convincing Eleonora that the plays she had previously appeared in were rubbish unworthy of her talents. She must refuse to act in such stuff. Bemused and overwhelmed by the powerful personality of this god among men, she agreed. In response to her timid inquiries about how she would live, the poet assured her that she would achieve both international fame and material security by appearing in his plays. To ensure this, all she needed to do was to invest what money she had in their production.

The game of cat and mouse which was to destroy Duse began. Whenever she had arranged to produce a play by D'Annunzio and was rehearsing it she was in favor. If the play failed she was to blame. If, to earn some money, she revived one of her past successes, she was rejected as a renegade and a traitor.

Eleonora kept up her hopeless struggle to hold D'Annunzio for almost twenty years—during which time she was as tortured as the Little Mermaid who loved a Prince. Her health declined, her nervous illnesses increased, she lost youth and vitality and declined into melancholy. Her stage appearances became rare, until, in 1914, she was forced into retirement at the age of fifty-five.

Duse made a final appearance in London and later in New York in 1923. Now almost too ill to act at all she was forced to do so or starve. She died while appearing in Pittsburgh in the winter of 1924. The description of those last days is pitiful. She was scarcely able to drag herself about, she was stupefied by the severity of the weather and quite unfitted for the task of being responsible for the Company. Her obsession for D'Annunzio had long since exhausted even the patience of those who had affection and regard for her and she was more truly alone than ever before. She collapsed and died among a Company almost as helpless and bewildered as she was herself.

Certainly D'Annunzio had other and more important matters to occupy his mind. The rise of fascism had

brought him fame as a patriot and poet. He had discarded
the waning star who died so unhappily in faraway Pittsburgh.

D'Annunzio survived Duse by fourteen years. He spent
his last ten years in a glow of publicity. He was a magnet
for tourists who, in the hope of getting a glimpse of the
great man, stood outside the fortress he had made his
home. Now he is remembered by only a handful of ad-
mirers. Their ardor, however, does not inspire them to
back expensive productions of his plays.

It is Duse who has become enshrined among the immortals, not because of her association with the poet of fascism but in spite of it. She was as truly exploited and
destroyed through the cult of the superman as any other
victim of the regime.

CHAPTER eighteen

A STUDY OF ELLEN TERRY

Of the internationally famous actresses whose private lives were as romantic as the roles they played on the stage, Ellen Terry lived the longest and remains the most enigmatical.

There is complete agreement between what almost everyone who knew Ellen Terry has recorded of her and the impression she made upon the public as an actress. Together these two impressions have created an indestructible legend. There is, however, a contradiction between this composite idea and some of the actual events in the life of the actress. If a psychologist who knew nothing of the legend were to plot her character from the meager information we have about her, he would show us a much more interesting person than the sugar-and-spice creature, congenitally young at heart, with whom we are familiar. Perhaps her ability to remain young at heart was an inherited characteristic, one that remained little influenced by realities. Certainly the majority of women who have had similar experiences have become disillusioned and later disinterested in romance. Ellen Terry did not. Even as an old woman she was still a romantic and still retained a fascination for the opposite sex.

Ellen's father was the son of an innkeeper at Portsmouth. He became an actor noted for his good looks and fine voice. His wife was Sarah Ballard, the daughter of a Scottish minister. She also possessed outstanding good looks and acting ability. Of their eleven children nine survived and all were connected with the theatre. It was the second child, Ellen, born in 1847, who became most famous.

Ellen made her first appearance on the London stage at the age of nine. She was a strikingly beautiful child with the luminously fair skin, red-gold hair and magnetic blue eyes that are a Terry heritage. Usually life is easier for the beautiful child than it is for the plain one. In those days there was no compulsory education and the girl was able to continue her life in the theatre without any serious interruptions by the demands of education. Does this provide a clue to the girl-who-would-not-grow-up during the seventy-odd years that still remained to her?

In 1863, when she was nearly sixteen, Ellen was playing in the Haymarket Theatre, London. It was then that she met G. F. Watts, the celebrated painter.

At that time the cultural life of England was enormously influenced by two men who, psychologically, had much in common—John Ruskin and G. F. Watts. Both men seem to have felt the call to lead humanity to higher things. Watts used his brush to this end, Ruskin his pen. Watts, although he was something of a hermit, noted for his humorless aestheticism, his gloom and lofty ideals, enjoyed a social following. He liked to mix with intellectuals, preferably those with an upper middle-class background. To his intimate circle he appears to have been something of a prophet and a seer as Ruskin was. Like Ruskin, his development seems to have been arrested at an immature emotional level and love affairs played no important part in his life. As a painter he was fabulously successful and had a large income.

Watts had no interest in or connection with the theatre. Yet during that season in 1863 when Ellen Terry was playing at the Haymarket Theatre he met and married her.

Perhaps to the artist, whose paintings suggest a deep preoccupation with the themes of love and death, the young girl may have seemed the very personification of youth and love. He may have believed that she could lead him out of the shades of his own personal underworld. On the other hand he may have wished her to reign there.

Ellen's reasons for marrying Watts are more obscure. Was she, like the child in the fairy tale, bored with her hitherto sunny existence, lured by the dark mystery of Watts' personality and the unknown world of aesthetic values which he had to offer her? This may have been so if one can judge by a passage in her memoirs about a meeting with E. W. Godwin before her marriage to Watts, when she was fifteen. She says, "For the first time I began to appreciate beauty, to observe, to feel the splendor of things, to *aspire*." Fifteen is an impressionable age and in view of Godwin's later place in Ellen's life he must have made a lasting impression on her. Did Ellen fall in love with Godwin's world—and later marry Watts because he belonged to this same world? Not only did he belong to it but he was far more famous and wealthy than Godwin ever was. Did Ellen's newly awakened aesthetic appreciations identify the man with the environment? Watts appears to have been an extremely impressive personality.

Lofty-mindedness was a quality much admired at that period and Watts' success is partly explained by the fact that he was living in the right place at the right time.

Whatever the explanation for the marriage, the results were unfortunate. The details are obscure except for some discreet and cautious comments made by observant guests at the painter's country home. We are told of a puzzled and timid young wife whom the middle-aged husband treated like a schoolgirl. Any display of youthful high spirits or fun was frowned upon. The pair was so incompatible that in less than a year they had separated. Within a very short time Ellen was living with Godwin, who was then in his thirties. Ellen did this despite the fact that after the parting with Watts she had been able to resume her stage career. She abandoned her career for the second time and for the second time also was lured by the appeal of another prominent figure in the current aesthetic movement. This time the relationship was more successful. It lasted for six years and there were two children, Edith, born in 1869, and Gordon in 1872. In his memories of his father, Gordon Craig is touchingly loving and affectionate. Like his mother, Gordon remains young in heart and it is as if the small boy in him never ceased to mourn the separation from a much loved father.

Although he was a less spectacular figure than Watts, Godwin was highly respected as an archeologist, an architect and a theatrical designer. In addition he seems to have had a very likable personality.

Ellen's account of her life with Godwin is curiously like a description of a Victorian lithograph. There is the rustic simplicity of background, the cottage with the roses round the door, and the young mother, little more than a child herself, with two beautiful children clinging to her knees. The record has little more reality than a dream, and the dreamlike quality persists in the description of an almost painless transition from rustic domesticity to the eventual resumption of a stage career in London.

This account is curiously different from the passages in Gordon Craig's last autobiography. Whatever the true situation may have been, the fact remains that after Watts divorced Ellen she married a man named Charles Kelly, a year later. Little is known of Kelly except that the marriage was short-lived and that he died in 1885.

Twelve months after she married Kelly a great change came about in Ellen's life. She met Henry Irving.

Like Watts and Godwin, Irving was a man with a mission. Of the three, Irving was the most masterful, the most sternly dedicated to his career and the most consistent in his single-minded purpose. When the famous partnership between Ellen Terry and Henry Irving began, she was twenty-eight and he was forty. Ellen was at an age when her immediate future was of extreme importance. She had twice abandoned her theatrical career, behind her was the marriage with Watts that had ended in divorce, the long romance with Godwin that had faded out, and another marriage that was already a failure.

Romance had played little part in Irving's life. He had married but the marriage was not a happy one and he seemed little interested in women. Perhaps it was to the theatre and not to any human being that Irving gave his heart. It is not clear whether Ellen realized this from the beginning or whether the realization only came to her gradually. Whatever may have been their reactions to each other in the first flush of joint success, Ellen was to write of Irving later that he was "quiet, patient, tolerant, impersonal, gentle, close, crafty, incapable of caring for anything outside his work." Eventually she was to say that Irving "cared for no one" and that this "is a pity."

When the long partnership ended, Ellen said she was the one to make the break and that she did so because there were so few parts in their old repertoire that she could still play after twenty years. On tour, therefore, she might only be able to appear in one or two roles. Yet it seems clear that Ellen was pained by the events that led to the end of the partnership and that the famous partners were never again on good terms with each other. It was about that time that she made the remark that Irving cared for no one. It may also be significant that although Charles Kelly had died in 1885, Ellen did not marry again until 1907, two years after Irving's death and some years after the partnership had been dissolved. It is true of some women that they can only give lasting allegiance to those whom they cannot conquer; perhaps this was true of Ellen Terry in her relationship with Irving.

To Ellen's son Gordon, Irving seems to have been a tower of strength in a world of shifting sands. It seems likely that to Ellen he was the same, despite her criticisms. It can scarcely be disputed that this was so as far as her career was concerned. Supporters of the two famous stars seem to incline to opposing viewpoints regarding Ellen's abilities. Irving enthusiasts held the opinion that Ellen Terry had never been a really great dramatic actress or capable of truly sustaining the great tragic parts she played with Irving. They maintained that she had good looks and charm and was pleasing in comedy roles. As regards good looks, charm and ability in comedy, Ellen had few detractors. On the contrary, as a personality she had a far larger and more adoring following than Irving ever had. Those who were and remained Irving enthusiasts were definitely in a minority after the partnership ended. It seemed that once old age and ill-health undermined Irving's power he lost his ascendancy over his audiences. Ellen never lost hers. The legend of her charm and fascination was too well established to be affected by time. Legends are tough and will withstand practically anything.

The nearest thing to criticism of Ellen's personality comes from a close relative who said, "Ellen is difficult, if not impossible to live with. Full of whims and caprice, generous, warmhearted and kind." Was the kindness the impulsive kindness of a child? Children can be thoughtless and sometimes, unintentionally, very cruel.

A curious light is thrown on Ellen in her old age through an incident told to me by someone who met her at a party organized to publicize one of her last series of appearances. An ardent supporter fallen, like Ellen, on hard days, organized this swan song. By now Ellen was partially blind and her memory for lines extremely unreliable. All the guests were waiting, eager to meet the great star. Time passed but the guest of honor did not arrive. Ellen had never been remarkable for her punctuality. Eventually a taxi drew up. The host hurried to the door and an imperious command came from inside the cab. "Get in and close the door. I want to talk to you." As soon as the door closed, the driver was told to drive on. It was two hours before Ellen had finished talking and the cab drew up at the house once more. Ellen alighted, her usual radiant self, projecting charm on such guests as were still present. Meanwhile her impecunious host settled the enormous taxi fare and wondered why business could not have been discussed inexpensively in his study.

Is there any thread to guide the explorer into the labyrinth that was Ellen Terry's soul? Only that the three men who played such significant parts in her life were all masterful personalities and much older than she was herself. Was her life, up to her middle age, dominated by her unconscious search for a father figure? Girls who refuse to grow up always need a father figure, and are likely to marry or be associated with older men. By substituting in turn Watts, Godwin and Irving for her father she was able to indefinitely postpone many of the burdens of maturity.

Ellen's greatest asset was her charm. Charm is a weapon suitable for both attack and defense. It can also propitiate. The famous critic J. T. Grein has left what is perhaps the best summary of the actress and also the woman:

> Hers is the exceptional gift of captivation. . . . She is always herself—which defines her possibilities and her limitations. By instinct and endowment Ellen Terry is a comedienne.

Certainly there is no other actress of similar status on whom the tragedy of broken human relationships seems to have sat so lightly. The legend has left us with a fairy-tale heroine dancing down the years in the magic world of the theatre. The irresistible child who found three fathers was also perhaps the eternal Narcissa enchanted by her own enchantments.

CHAPTER nineteen

MODERN SOCIAL DEVELOPMENTS AND THE THEATRE

It is difficult for any art to keep pace with developments in the society to which it is linked. In the theatre this is a particularly difficult problem because its life line is dependent on box office returns and it dare not go far ahead of public opinion. The most successful playwright is the one whose work stays at least one jump ahead of public opinion; the play has to be understood, to some extent, by the slowest as well as the quickest minds in the audience. Bernard Shaw was probably the most successful exponent of the delicate art of leading public opinion without getting too far ahead of it. For years past, however, many English plays have been far behind the times. When a well-written play dealing with some aspect of contemporary life is staged, the critics almost utter a prayer. Even when there are technical defects or inadequacies the critics may still recommend the play.

Promoters of plays know little of art as a rule and still less of cultural or social developments. To the speculator, sex is still the pot of gold at the end of the theatrical rainbow. That there is some truth in this assumption can scarcely be denied but it does not follow that, because the work of a playwright who writes on this theme seriously and has something to say is a success, some vulgar, inept and artificial treatment of the same theme will be equally successful.

Many British plays suffer from lack of vitality and intellectual anemia rather than blatant vulgarity. I think this is one reason why so many of them fail on Broadway. One explanation of this failure heard over here is that tastes are so different. Yet the best American plays are a resounding success here, which suggests that tastes are not so very different. In northern Europe, where there are flourishing theatres but an insufficient number of native playwrights to keep them going, many translated plays are performed. At one time the majority of these were from English playwrights and numerically may still be so. But the number of American plays performed is rising and audiences often prefer them because they feel that they are more democratic in theme and therefore more significant than many English plays.

The theatre is of course passing through a phase when so-called realism is the fashion. There is, however, a good deal of confusion about the meaning of this word. Realism of presentation is simply one method by which the playwright expresses *what* he has to say but it does not make what he has to say more true or profound. In fact realism of presentation may sometimes be a mask for poverty of ideas or lack of integrity. So-called realism in acting may be equally misleading. Every change in the manner of acting has been thought of as an advance in realism. This was what Shakespeare was calling for when he wrote the Players' speech for *Hamlet*. He believed that the players of his time were making an advance toward realistic acting. David Garrick prided himself on a similar achievement, as did Mrs. Siddons. Kean was thought to be one of the great realistic actors of his day and aroused envy and jealousy in older actors who believed that they had been masters of realism. Henry Irving believed that he had made further advances in realistic acting. Bernard Shaw did not believe that Irving had done so and made noisy claims to his own influence in this direction. He believed that as a result of his association with the productions of Granville-Barker, realism in the theatre could go no further.

Yet when Ireland's Abbey Theatre came into being, its director, W. B. Yeats, was so scornful of what he called the artificiality of English acting that he insisted he could only get what he wanted by having no professional players and he chose raw amateurs. Many years later when, as a young theatre critic on a Dublin weekly paper, I saw the Abbey Players, I was deeply impressed by them. At that time they still had Sara Allgood, F. J. McCormack, Barry Fitzgerald, and several others of considerable talent. Here were people creating an illusion of contemporary human beings. When I returned to Dublin fifteen years later and the players mentioned had gone, the realism had fossilized into mannered rigidity. Perhaps this had happened through lack of new talent. The abiding truth may be that it is only through the actor's individual attainments that great art will stay with us and that the *manner* of its presentation by either playwright or actor is of secondary importance.

The star system is often blamed for the poor quality of many plays. It is true to some extent that the play of ideas is likely to demand a high standard of teamwork rather than a star in the leading role supported by a collection of average players. It is natural that the play with a star part should have the greatest appeal to the child-who-wants-to-be-king. It is also true, however, that a number of plays that are deeply concerned with contemporary problems have provided stars with very fat parts. So it does not seem that the play of ideas and contemporary problems need necessarily exclude parts worthy of the star.

Before condemning the egotism of the star it must be remembered that it served a purpose. The actor's passionate obsession to act in spectacular parts which have a simple, direct appeal to the public, together with his indifference to everything that does not immediately impinge on his professional existence, has helped the theatre to survive through its most difficult periods. What this narrow interest does not do is keep drama fresh and virile. Nor does it necessarily provide the individual actor with the fullest opportunities to develop into a great artist. In contrast to both the United States and Great Britain, the French theatre is more intellectually advanced.

Ever since the French Revolution the intellectuals have seen the theatre as a platform for ideas, and of course the French people respect learning and do not despise the intellectual. As a result Paris—like New York—has two types of theatre, but unlike New York, experimental or controversial plays are not necessarily relegated to small or unfashionable theatres. Nor are the plays performed by struggling actors but by the greatest of the French stars. Among the best known of these are Louis Barrault and Gerard Phillip.

Few French plays are a great success in England with the exception of those of Anouilh. It is interesting that for years this dramatist was regarded as a "Boulevard" playwright, that is, his plays were performed in the commercial theatres. This is not an indication that all French plays are of a higher intellectual standard than those of the United States or Great Britain. On the contrary, many popular offerings in Paris are bedroom farces or their like which sink to a banality unknown in America or England.

It is doubtful however if the French plays most concerned with ideas could be popular outside France, for they usually lack humanity. It is significant that one very successful French play, which was also most successful in its short run at the London Arts Theatre, was written by Julian Green, who is a "French American." The play is set in the Southern States at the time of the Civil War. Because the leading character was a homosexual, it was only licensed in England for performance in a club theatre. Everyone who saw the play, including the professional critics, was so enthusiastic about it that every effort was made to secure permission for a transfer to a large theatre but without success. In *South* the author seemed to combine the strength of French intellect with the emotional force of the best type of American dramatist.

The existence of the theatre has never been jeopardized by lack of acting talent but through lack of good plays. The great social changes after 1918 saw the emergence of American playwrights who welcomed social changes. British playwrights did not and—like many of their audiences —pined for a return of "the good old days." Up to the outbreak of the second World War, few plays of any great importance had been written even by new English playwrights. During the years 1930 to 1939, plays in London theatres came, failed and vanished so fast that it was difficult to keep track of them. Theatre managements sought a solution for their troubles by staging more and more comedies, including revivals of the classics. After the second war a new technological and social revolution began —a revolution which has left British playwrighting far behind. The people of the theatre, however, seem to have remained blissfully unconscious that the theatre, instead of being in the forefront of more enlightened opinion, lags far behind the stage of development reached by the average intelligent industrial technician.

The great age of speculation in plays passed thirty years ago. The more astute of the speculators gambled in film-making instead. Between the two world wars hundreds of English theatres were converted into cinemas. In the United States, theatre began to recede until it could be found in only a few large cities. There were many Americans who solemnly believed that live theatre was not only vanishing but was "out of date," in the same way that magic-lantern shows were out of date. Now the wheel has come full circle in England. Many cinemas have been closed and a few have been turned into theatres. If a theatre does go out of business, no one in their senses would dream of turning it into a cinema. Cinema attendances are still falling in Great Britain and, of course, in the United States. What is the significance of this trend and what has brought it about?

The actor will like to think that the public has come to a new appreciation of the theatre because stage acting has improved its standards. He will say that in the long run live theatre must have a greater appeal than synthetic entertainment. This conviction may be partly true but it does not account for what is happening, because there are thousands of people in Great Britain and an even larger number in the United States who have never seen live theatre in their lives.

The cinema has declined in popularity for the same reason that the theatre declined after the first World War. The cinema industry of 1946 was just as blinded by prosperity as the theatrical business of 1918. It lagged behind general social developments.

In Great Britain the New Industrial Revolution crept up unnoticed, partly because all change was ascribed to political rather than economic developments. Yet in the United States, where political power moved to the Right instead of the Left, social changes not only took the same trends as those in Great Britain but outdistanced them.

American sociologists were the first to give some interesting information about the results of the new revolution. These results have had, and will continue to have, the most far-reaching effects in the theatre and on the lives of everyone connected with it.

Increased prosperity and a higher general standard of education, to meet the expanding technological developments, have transformed the cultural pattern of the United States. To a lesser extent the same process is going on in Great Britain.

Overlong working hours for most working people are a thing of the past. The working day is shorter and the five-day week is the rule rather than the exception. Since people are less tired and more mentally alert than ever before, they are becoming more critical of the standards of their entertainment. Television is not the only explanation of the fact that film production is about a third of what it was and that the figure is still decreasing. In America there seems to be some reason for the belief that television has passed the highest peak of its prosperity because the quality of the entertainment provided has not kept pace with its mechanical developments.

Because cinema and television, and also some types of

commercial theatre, lack what the public needs, all three are less popular than they were. In addition, new energies and new needs have made these pastimes less important than other things. What do people spend their time and money on today?

In Great Britain, foreign travel comes first. Also the "do-it-yourself" movement is at least as popular as it is in the United States. Allied with this is a desire to learn handicrafts and painting. Yet the performance of dramatic plays, whether by amateurs or professionals, does meet social and emotional needs more satisfactorily than any other pastime. This is obvious in the proliferation of theatre movements of all kinds going on in the United States at the present time. In England there are now signs of similar stirrings, even though these are concurrent with the closing of larger numbers of provincial repertory theatres than ever before. It must be remembered, however, that many of these theatres are either large, old buildings that are decaying, uncomfortable and expensive to run, or else they are too small and very dilapidated. Running costs are too high for rebuilding to be undertaken.

Whether or not the actor believes that the theatre is entering a period of increased prosperity, he certainly hopes so for he does not easily adapt himself to acting in other mediums. He may be glad to earn some money at film acting but he prefers the theatre. He regards acting for radio as a poor substitute for appearing on the stage and his attitude to television is at best ambivalent. He is aware that the publicity value of television appearances is enormous but he prefers direct contact with his audience. In this the British actor is more conservative than his opposite number in the United States, but of course tradition plays its part here.

Thousands of young actors have grown up in the United States without ever seeing a live stage performance. To them acting means acting for films or television. Also, they are likely to have come raw to their craft, particularly in acting for films, so they have neither the problem of discarding a technique that has become second nature nor conflict in learning what is needed for acting for the cinema or television screens.

American stage players with training and experience have the same preference for acting in a theatre as the British actor has. There are technical as well as other factors involved. As every stage actor knows, the audience is part of the play and there is an uncanny link between the actor and his audience. He is aware during every moment of his performance just how the audience is reacting not only to his performance as a whole but to the way he speaks a line or even a word. He gets enormous reassurance when (or where) he knows all is going well. He has the opportunity to change his acting or delivery at any point where he feels the response to be less good. By repeated performances he can experiment until he knows the audience is completely with him for every minute of his appearance on stage. This situation cannot exist in the case of film, radio or television performances.

That the members of an audience should be able to participate in this way is as important for them as it is for the actor. Unfortunately they are less aware of this process of participation than the players on the stage and only dimly realize their loss when they are deprived of a theatre.

An alarming trend in Great Britain has been the pulling down of a number of theatres in large cities and the utilization of their sites for other purposes. Actors are inclined to blame the business ineptitude of the profession for this. Yet it seems doubtful if poor business management is entirely responsible for the demolition of theatre buildings. The plain truth is that even at its best, theatrical enterprise of any kind could not be the most profitable type of commercial enterprise under present-day conditions. So if the owner of a theatre building is solely concerned with the size of his profits, then sooner or later that theatre will be demolished however successful it may be. The same would be true of any building devoted to the intangibles; that is, any form of art or even education. London's National Gallery is situated in the heart of London and on what must be one of the most valuable sites in the metropolis. Had it been privately owned it would have been pulled down long ago to make way for a more profitable undertaking. The same fate would overtake the galleries and museums in New York or any other large city. As far as the theatre is concerned its problems can only be solved when it enjoys the same protection it has been accorded in many European countries for hundreds of years. In such countries it has been realized that man cannot live by bread alone, but in the two most technologically advanced countries in the world today—the United States and Great Britain—there seems to be an increasing tendency to believe that man can live by dividends alone.

Fortunately the real people of the theatre have not got such confused values. If they had, the vital off-Broadway theatres would not exist in the numbers they do today nor would the struggling repertory companies that are still to be found in the English provinces.

It must be realized, however, that in the age of the Second Industrial Revolution the theatre is still attempting to carry on under the same economic system as in the age of Shakespeare or Garrick. The fact is, a flourishing theatre art cannot be run as a commercial proposition any more than a school or a church can be. Nor will theatre art suffer as a result of subsidy of some kind. Holland has one of the finest theatre movements in the world. Municipalities lose no money by giving it their support and the Government gets back most of what it spends on the theatre through taxes. It is more economical to have a flourishing theatre with rates and taxes being paid by all concerned than to be paying out large sums of money in relief for unemployed actors.

In Great Britain, subsidies administered through the Arts Council have been of vital importance to the entertainment world more particularly in opera and ballet, which could scarcely exist without this aid. The theatre receives smaller sums from the Arts Council but a little help is given by some local authorities. Permission for these authorities to give grants was obtained some years ago, but direction rather than permission is what is needed. It was optimistic to suppose that when given freedom to spend money on the theatre or to salt it away, most local authorities would not prefer the latter course. Most of these officials know little and care less about the theatre.

Despite all this the British actor is usually opposed to subsidies or help from the state. Like the American, he has a prejudice against state—or municipal—control of any kind. This tendency is of course shared by the man in the street as well. Yet once changes have come about, all accept them. No one would now seriously suggest that education could get along under private enterprise, that armies should be manned by mercenaries, that the post office should cease to be a government department or that public libraries should be abolished. It seems clear that the British Broadcasting Corporation is looked upon as a lesser evil than commercial radio and television. Even in the United States there is now a suspicion that an organization similar to the B.B.C. might be worth consideration. People are beginning to ask themselves if it might not be more truly democratic to have more public ownership and less private monopoly in entertainment. There is only one valid criterion for criticism of any organization, whoever handles it, and that is, does it work efficiently?

Despite crippling prejudices there are people in the theatrical profession who realize that the theatre cannot fulfill its function while run on present commercial lines and who believe that the system followed in Holland would stabilize our theatre both in Great Britain and the United States, give better artistic results, and save waste of talent and money. Yet many fear any sort of liaison with state or municipality. They feel that either authority is only waiting to have the doors opened to them in order to smother the theatre in red tape. The truth is, of course, that just as there was a hard fight in Great Britain to get such subsidies as now exist, there would be a longer and harder fight to get legislation for any such plan as the Dutch Theatre plan. That any official body would, in addition, be willing to spend money on an enormous force of officials to see that the theatre was "tied up in red tape" is not very rational.

In Holland the profession runs its own affairs through the co-ordination of all theatre enterprises. This organization does have to account for the way it handles its financial budget as a whole, but it does not have to take orders from above as to how the money is spent.

Some theatre people favor help along the lines of patronage from big business firms. As and when such firms care to give money to the theatre this is not to be despised —all help is welcome. But such haphazard charity is not suitable for modern conditions. Insofar as actors see private patronage as a solution to economic problems in the theatre they are only providing further confirmation of their tendency to live in the past.

CHAPTER twenty

THE ACTOR IN THE NEW
SOCIETY

When the chaotic economy of commercial enterprise in the theatre of the United States and Great Britain has been replaced by a less wasteful system, then the theatre in both countries should come nearer to being what all those who love it would wish it to be. There should be more good plays, more theatres and more employment.

It may be asked where the audiences for this expanded theatre are to come from. Research in Great Britain and in the United States indicates the answers.

The lower the cultural and economic standards of a given population, the more it inclines to passivity. Entertainments that make very little demand on the spectator are preferred. Spectacles of one kind or another are popular even when they are far from first-rate. Box office returns for inferior entertainment of this kind passed their peak some years ago. As the worker rises from unskilled to skilled occupations his taste in entertainment changes. With constant advances in technology the unskilled will no longer form the broad base of the population in highly industrialized countries. The unskilled will tend to become a minority because the society of the Second Industrial Revolution will have no place for them.

Higher education will influence taste. Interest is already declining in entertainments which rely solely on sexual appeal as well as in any art form which presents sexual activity as the most important of all activities. There are potential audiences for better theatre.

The play of ideas is beginning to have a wider appeal. These ideas must of course be related to life as experienced by many people and not by an elite minority. It would seem that the more highly industrialized a modern state becomes, the more classless its society will be. In a classless society the playwright is better able to find basic themes for his plays and so can appeal to wider audiences. One example of this is to be noticed in the success in England of the Australian play *The Summer of the Seventeenth Doll*. The men in this play are cane cutters but the play is not simply about cane cutters any more than *The Death of a Salesman* is solely concerned with salesmen. Profound issues are the real basis of both plays, problems that are part of industrialized society, problems that have no connection with "class."

Because Britain is not yet a classless society both playwright and actor are in a curious situation. The artist in a class society will naturally be drawn toward the class with whom he feels he has most in common; that is, the middle class. In the past the British playwright knew that he had to provide entertainment which would appeal to the social attitudes of the middle and upper classes. These were the people who occupied the most expensive seats in the theatre and the larger number of seats as well.

At that time the working classes occupied the cheapest seats, which were in the gallery, and gallery audiences were content to accept plays that pleased their betters. In recent years the situation has changed. Prosperity enables the working classes to buy themselves more expensive seats when they do go to a theatre and many an "h" is now dropped in the dress circle. Good musicals attract these patrons but they are also góing to good plays in greater numbers. The plays that attract the younger ones have themes which are concerned with contemporary life as they know it. There are still too few plays of this kind. The majority of plays ignore social changes and contemporary problems.

The prevalence of plays with outmoded plots has certainly contributed to the failure of many theatrical companies, to the closing down of hundreds of theatres and to the tremendous rise in unemployment in the acting profession.

The cause of unemployment in the United States is rather different. There industrial expansion was so rapid that provision of "live" entertainment has never had a chance to keep pace. There are thousands of people who have never seen a play. However, it would be an oversimplification to suggest that the problems of the actor are going to be solved merely through the provision of a vast number of theatres throughout the United States. In many ways society in the United States has less need of the theatre than is the case in Great Britain. In spite of increased spending power, class distinctions still inhibit the Briton from full enjoyment of the fruits of his labor. It is not enough for the Briton to know that he can afford to have a meal in an expensive hotel, if he is haunted by the knowledge that he (or she) behaves differently, speaks differently, and perhaps dresses differently than the other patrons. There is the fear or at least the suspicion that the waiter will register awareness of this even if nobody else does. So a jaunt to a theatre is safer.

In the United States, the only thing anyone has to ask himself is whether he can afford an outing. In a broader context, any American mother may cherish a dream that her son may one day become President. No English mother could indulge in a dream about her son becoming the ruler of Great Britain unless she was of royal blood.

An English actor who has worked in the United States said to me, "Americans are less theatre-minded than the British because they are more extroverted. In one way they are all actors. They are all conscious of playing a part in the never-ending drama of American development and expansion. The intense competition and struggle for success are in themselves dramatic."

There is probably a great deal of truth in this view but the fact remains that the struggle for success is taking a slightly different form. Participation in cultural activities becomes part of the life pattern of the successful man and now it is also becoming part of the pattern for those who are improving their lot. Few people who see even a small number of interesting plays manage to remain proof against the deep primitive attraction the theatre has for mankind. American actors with whom I have discussed this point seem to feel confident that given the opportunity to see plays the American people will become more interested in the theatre. They think that in some places this interest will develop rapidly and in others more slowly and that as it does, there are both the plays and the players to meet the demand.

In Great Britain, there is a larger percentage of theatres in relation to the total population than in the United

States although so many have closed. It may be that the situation in Britain will further deteriorate for a short time. West End theatre managements are lacking in vision and with a few rare exceptions provincial managements are the tail attached to the West End kite. In England there has never been a theatre that could compare with the American Group Theatre in vision and enterprise nor with the off-Broadway theatres of today. It is true that London has had the Arts Theatre for years, the Court Theatre for several years and at the time of writing the newly opened Mermaid Theatre. So far, however, these theatres have had to get along without real stars because few of the leading stars are enterprising enough to appear in any theatre outside the West End however unusual the plays staged in the smaller theatres may be. It is to be hoped that the social changes which are under way and the effect they must have on taste in drama will gradually be realized by everyone in the British theatre. Those who are at the top should give the leadership that is necessary if the theatre is to expand along the lines that will enable it to share in the prosperity of the new society.

It may well be that in both Great Britain and the United States a form of theatre which already exists in both countries will play a significant part in the theatre of the future. In the United States these theatres have been called community theatres and they exist in towns which may have no other form of theatre. In Great Britain such theatres tend to find their homes in suburbs of large cities, and although they do not call themselves community theatres, this is what they really are. As is the case with the American ones, the casts are not professional although they may have professional directors.

One of the most important functions of the community theatre is that it can provide the playwright with an opportunity to learn his craft and the technique of his art. Such knowledge can be acquired only through working in a theatre in some capacity. In the past many people whose real interest was in playwrighting managed to obtain some sort of work in the professional theatre, but that is becoming increasingly difficult. Competition in the acting profession is now so intense that only those who have spent some years in training at a drama school can hope to obtain an engagement. Even if he were willing to spend a couple of years in a drama school, the would-be playwright might be unacceptable because his talent and psychological traits would not be those of the student solely interested in acting.

In England there have always been actors who have taken up playwrighting, but when the professional actor of some years' experience does this there is always the danger that his plays may be rich in showy acting parts but poor in content. A play needs to be "good theatre" in order to be entertaining, but a play that is merely theatrical may be very poor entertainment.

As regards other kinds of employment apart from acting, this is almost impossible to obtain because it calls for technical training and knowledge.

It is ironical that while members of a modern professional theatre company have to be highly trained, the person whose work is the foundation upon which they must build is all too often an amateur. Most plays on which options are taken have to be altered, cut here and expanded there before they are staged. Some are practically rewritten. Few plays would ever reach the stage if this were not done. Unfortunately, such a procedure does not ensure that the results are as good as if the playwright were able to write his play in accordance with the technical requirements in the first place. Like a painting a play is—or should be—a complete work of art. No painter would accept an offer for one of his works on the understanding that he should alter it as required and perhaps even allow others to do some of the alterations for him.

Quite apart from the demands of technique, there is another reason for alterations of plays. That is the demands of the star who may be appearing in the play. A star can often influence changes in a script which do not make for a better play but for a bigger star part. It is not unusual for stars to insist on the removal of witty or forceful lines from other parts in order that they may be added to the star's lines. They will inflate their own role at the expense of other players and often to the detriment of the play as a whole. Or they may insist on cuts in other people's lines with the same end in view.

Managements pander to the stars because they believe that a star can make a success of any play, even a weak one. They persist in this belief in spite of the fact that every year on Broadway or Shaftesbury Avenue there are a number of resounding failures to disprove this theory.

More community theatres might go a long way toward solving the problems of the playwright. In the United States, many have existed for years and they have helped playwrights, but more are needed in Great Britain. A playwright may get some help of course from seeing his first efforts tried out by purely amateur groups who hire a hall or a small theatre for one or two nights several times a year. The drawback in such a procedure is that audiences for such groups are usually drawn from friends and relatives of the players who come to see the show in an uncritical spirit. These audiences expect so little that what is really worth seeing in the show may be unappreciated, just as the bits that deserve criticism are tolerantly passed over. Apart from all this, amateur players who have had no training and who are directed by an amateur are not usually fitted to reveal to the budding playwright what is good, bad or even superfluous in his play. Another important point in the development of the playwright is for him to see his play performed for at least a week, not for just one or two performances.

Whatever changes take place in the theatre of the future, it is certain that increasingly high standards will be necessary. Waste will have to be eliminated and at present a prime source of waste is the play that is a flop. Playwrights will have to have something significant to say and will need to know how to say it if they really hope to eliminate the danger of any of their plays being dismal failures.

Managements will need to judge a play on its own merits as entertainment and not accept weak plays because they can see in them a showy vehicle for stars they happen to have under contract.

Most important of all, actors will need to re-educate themselves so that they can detect (and accept) the difference between a good play and a good star part.

For psychological reasons the star system has an innate appeal to the actor, and the more competitive the society in which he lives the greater his desire for stardom. He does not realize that the total impact on the audience of a play in which every player gets a fair chance to show what he can do is the lifeblood of the theatre. Those whose talents are the most outstanding will still get the appreciation they deserve. This happens in countries where a built-in star system does not exist. Outstanding players have a following to pay them homage. But their followers pay them this homage in the theatre and not by congregating in screaming hordes at railway stations when a favorite actor arrives or outside a hotel where he is staying.

If the dinosaur of commercial theatre vanishes from our world because economic changes have made it unsuitable and impractical, the acting profession will find itself in a more healthy state. Stars may not have such inflated salaries for the periods during which they are performing, but the total sum of their real earnings over a lifetime in the theatre may be much the same. They will pay less in taxes and on their way to the top they will not experience long periods of unemployment. Neither will they have to fear the possibility of decline in middle age or old age through the "slings and arrows of outrageous fortune" that may beset them in the cutthroat competition of purely commercial theatre. They will also know that they will not have to appear in poor plays or in any one play for an inordinately long run.

Inflated star salaries are only one of the economic factors that make theatrical enterprise difficult under present-day conditions in commercial theatre. Inflated theatre rents are often crippling. Then there are the problems of high salaries for members of the backstage staff who are protected by powerful trade unions. In industry the less skilled workers would not expect to receive larger salaries than skilled key workers, but at the present time a stage hand may have to be paid nearly three times the minimum salary for an actor in the United States, and in Great Britain at least as much as is paid in minimum salary to the actor who is touring or appearing in the West End. In both countries this has resulted in the almost total disappearance of the road show, once one of the most flourishing sectors of theatrical entertainment.

All overhead expenses are high in the theatre. In the United States, one reason for the popularity of summer theatre, from the viewpoint of the managements, is that heating of the theatre buildings is not necessary. If it were necessary, the small margin of profit might be wiped out.

A progressive idea that may play a large part in the expansion of the theatre in the future is the creation of the municipal arts center. In such centers we shall not only have the municipal theatre, long established on the continent of Europe, but we shall have along with it an art gallery, a concert hall, and lecture rooms. This plan is not unknown in the United States, but it is essential for its success, both there and in Great Britain, that the theatre and concert hall should be leased to professional artists for a large part of the year. Interest in the arts can only be aroused and sustained if citizens are given the opportunity of enjoying the best that is available.

At present there is a deep chasm between the amateur and the professional in all the arts and this can cause jealousy, ill-feeling and lack of co-operation. But in the future, increased leisure will offer the amateur opportunities to reach higher standards.

In the United States, the amateur actor has been well served as far as accommodation is concerned. It has been suggested by some American critics with whom I have discussed this matter that the very good material conditions available to many nonprofessional groups in the United States are responsible for neglect of the vital necessities in any theatre production. These critics say that too little attention is paid to the training of the players as actors both technically and in an understanding of their art, and that directors tend to be glorified stage managers. This is certainly the case in regard to some of the more prosperous amateur companies in Great Britain. They invariably put on a play which has run in the West End, they hire a theatre, hire the set used in the West End—

or a replica of it—and the costumes also if costumes are required. They have all the trappings but none of the essentials of good theatre.

Greater accomplishment is shown by students of evening institutes who are given a full dramatic training and directed by professional directors. It is the training that is most important, because a man who is simply called in to direct amateurs in a play has little time to improve their individual acting abilities.

If amateurs both in Great Britain and the United States can be provided with training at reasonable fees, the present gap between the professional and nonprofessional theatre will lessen considerably. Then out-of-work professional actors or former professionals who have taken up other employment will be more willing to appear on the same stage with the amateur.

Among players in the United States there is a great desire for repertory theatres. It is to be hoped that those who wish to foster such a plan will do their utmost to get some first-hand knowledge in England of repertory as it is rather than plunge head-on into its problems. It would be a great pity if the more undesirable aspects of English repertory were to be perpetuated elsewhere. The plain truth is that if a repertory theatre has to operate on a purely commercial basis it can fail artistically if not financially. The threat of the latter is likely to lead to the realities of the former.

A repertory theatre must be accommodated in a building which is obtainable at a very reasonable rent. This rent is only reasonable when it can be based on an assessment of the actual expenses and *probable* profits of the Company, and not on the assumption that the theatre will be at least three-quarters full every evening. At present many repertory theatres can only cover their costs by twice-nightly performances. When these are combined with the production of a new play every week, the results are artistically disastrous.

Some managements have tried to raise their standards by interchanging companies—that is, the same company will play for one week in three towns within reasonable distance of each other. Such a scheme needs careful planning and can best be done when the same management runs two or three theatres and signs up enough players to provide each theatre with the necessary cast at the same salary for each theatre. Otherwise, players find themselves performing at varying salaries in each town. Accommodation is another problem because if the players interchange lodgings, the standards and cost of the lodgings may vary. The best solution to this would be if all such theatres had accommodation for the company. At present only one theatre, the Belgrade at Coventry, has this.

Whatever scheme is worked out, two bugbears of British repertory should be avoided. First, the weekly change of play and secondly, the producer-actor. I have visited many repertory theatres. In all cases the really good ones had a director who did not act, or who only occasionally acted one small part because his cast was not large enough to cover a certain play.

When Americans talk about repertory they almost invariably refer to the Abbey Theatre in Dublin, where a play runs for at least three weeks as a general rule. Salaries in the Abbey were low in the past, so low that many of the players did other jobs during the day. If this had not been so the theatre could not have continued to exist. In recent years, salaries have been a little better but still low by either British or American standards. Also, the theatre has had a small subsidy from the state for some years.

The success of the Abbey Theatre should reassure

American and British actors who so fear state subsidies. The Irish Free State Government has not interfered with the Abbey in any way detrimental to its existence, whereas in both Britain and the United States the theatre is often hamstrung by businessmen and methods belonging to a past age. This will always be so when profits made in the theatre do not go back into the theatre.

Another safeguard which actors on both sides of the Atlantic are reluctant to accept is regulated entry into the profession. Naturally they are backed in this attitude by the commercial managements, whose power would be much reduced if more than half the profession were not out of work at any one time.

Nevertheless, in talking to American players I have found in them a pioneer spirit and an idealistic enthusiasm about the future of their theatre. Perhaps they may draw additional strength from the knowledge that neither the theatre nor the acting profession will ever die out. The actor has made a long journey already—out of the jungle, through the temple, into the church and out of it again. He has been a mummer in the market place and the lord of the playhouse. He has known the radio, the cinema and television. Yet the road still stretches before him and will do so as long as civilization exists. Today the theatre is about to take a great move forward, together with new and larger audiences from among the mass of the people who are helping to create the world of the future.